A Message from the Drug Enforcement Administration

Increasingly the news is full of reports providing misleading or biased information about our nation's drug policies. Whether there are questions about the Drug Enforcement Administration's (DEA) actions to enforce federal law, or challenges to the basic concept that drugs are dangerous, there is a growing discussion as to whether our current drug policies are effective and appropriate.

This booklet, *Speaking Out Against Drug Legalization*, is designed to cut through the current fog of misinformation with hard facts. It presents an accurate picture of America's experience with drug use, the nature of the drug problem, and the potential for damage if the United States adopts a more permissive policy on drug abuse. The information is presented in a bulleted format, in an effort to provide specific points in response to the most common myths and facts about drugs and drug abuse.

Drug abuse, and this nation's response to it, is one of the most important and complex challenges facing all Americans—especially our youth. The national drug policies presently in place were not dreamed up from an ivory tower of idealism, but instead were constructed from the cold realities of experience.

From a historical perspective, the unique freedoms offered by the United States have always depended on a well-informed public. Accordingly, the DEA hopes you will use the scrupulously researched facts you find in this booklet to help you educate your friends and family.

A Message from the International Association of Chiefs of Police

Every year, the use and abuse of drugs kills tens of thousands of Americans and condemns countless others to a life of addiction, misery and pain. Yet, despite these horrific statistics, there is a broad scale effort underway to "legalize" illegal narcotics in communities and states throughout the country. All too often, supporters of these initiatives mislead the public about the impact of drug legalization and ignore the harm that the wide spread use of narcotics will have on a community.

The simple truth is that legalizing narcotics will not make life better for our citizens, ease the level of crime and violence in our communities nor reduce the threat faced by law enforcement officers. To suggest otherwise ignores reality.

There is a reason why the International Association of Chiefs of Police (IACP) and every major law enforcement organization opposes efforts at drug legalization or decriminalization. We are public safety experts who have witnessed first-hand the damage and horror that drug abuse visits on society. We have witnessed the lost promise of a child who becomes addicted to drugs and whose life descends into the never-ending hell of dependency and squalor. We have viewed the pain and anguish on the faces of parents and relatives who have lost a loved one to a drug overdose.

Far from being an answer to these problems, drug legalization will condemn tens of thousands of our fellow citizens to a life of dependency and horror and endanger the lives of countless innocent others who share the roads and their communities.

This publication is an invaluable resource which provides law enforcement executives and officers, elected officials, community leaders, teachers, parents and all those who are concerned about community safety with the information and resources they need in order to accurately inform the public of the dangers of drug legalization.

Table of Contents

SPEAKING OUT
Against Drug Legalization

Popular

Myths

About Drug Legalization

1 "The enforcement of drug laws contributes to violence along the Southwest border."

- Some have proposed legalizing drug consumption in the United States as a way to reduce border violence. This ignores scientific, legal, and social arguments that highlight what legalizing drugs would cost the United States, and that marijuana legalization would be a failed law enforcement strategy for both the United States and Mexico.

  - Criminals won't stop being criminals if we make drugs legal. Individuals who have chosen to pursue a life of crime and violence aren't likely to change course, get legitimate jobs, and become honest, tax-paying citizens just because we legalize drugs. The individuals and organizations that smuggle drugs don't do so because they enjoy the challenge of "making a sale." They sell drugs because that's what makes them the most money.

  - The violence in Mexico is a reflection of a larger battle as to whether Mexico will be governed under the rule of law, or the rule of the gun. We should take steps to reduce the killings by the drug cartels in Mexico and along our Southwest border, but suggesting that legalizing dope is going to make a difference in this effort makes no sense. The fight in Mexico is over money, and not just money generated by drugs, but for any illegal activity where profits can be made.

- Drug-related violence in Mexico is not a fight over market access or distribution chains in the United States, but the result of major Mexican drug trafficking organizations vying for control of both the drug smuggling routes leading into and out of Mexico, and transportation corridors along the border.

- Marijuana is only a part of the illegal drug traffic moving between Mexico and the United States. Changing the status of marijuana in the United States will not stop drug traffickers' motivations for moving drugs to U.S. markets. Remember, drug traffickers do what they do for money, not for altruistic reasons. Regardless of the legal status of marijuana, there will still be profits to be made in other drugs, guns, people, or other contraband. Just as organized crime didn't end when alcohol prohibition in the U.S. was lifted in 1933 *(see section on prohibition, page 58)*, drug trafficking and its associated violence isn't going to dissipate if the United States decides to legalize marijuana.

- In 2008, according to the Interagency Assessment of Cocaine Movement, approximately 90 percent of the cocaine destined for the United States transited the Mexico/Central America corridor—an estimated 16.8 metric tons of cocaine entered the United States by way of the Southwest border.

- According to DEA intelligence estimates, 80 percent of the methamphetamine consumed in the U.S. now comes from Mexico-based drug trafficking organizations. Methamphetamine seizures along the Southwest border have increased from 1,170 kilograms in CY 2001 to 2,232 kilograms in CY 2008, a 91-percent increase.

- The National Drug Intelligence Center estimates that Mexican and Colombian Drug Trafficking Organizations generate, remove, and launder between $18 billion and $39 billion in wholesale drug proceeds annually, a large portion of which is believed to be bulk-smuggled out of the United States over the Southwest border. [1]

- Enforcement efforts make a positive difference in reducing drug-related violence. First, it makes it harder for traffickers to move their product. Over the last 18 months, price and purity data collected by the DEA show the price of methamphetamine and cocaine is up, while the purity of these same drugs is down. Intelligence reporting confirms that trafficking organizations are having problems moving product into the United States, and the demand is such that they are able to charge more for a weaker product. While law enforcement efforts along the Southwest border, in the Caribbean, and in Mexico have seen repeated successes, there have been no significant changes in demand reduction activities in the United States.

- A comprehensive strategy addressing drug use and trafficking from all angles can and does make a difference. DEA supports an effective, comprehensive national drug control strategy, and we are working with the Department of Justice and the Office of National Drug Control Policy as they develop this strategy.

- We need to be aware of the nature of addiction itself and support research in this key area. We should continue to be advocates for effective and proven prevention efforts that reduce drug abuse and addiction. We must provide treatment for those that need it, and we must enforce our nation's drug laws which fundamentally help protect our citizens and communities.

2 "Legalizing and taxing marijuana will help local economies by reduceing crime and increasing tax revenue."

- Marijuana is a dangerous, mind-altering drug. That's the conclusion the Food and Drug Administration (FDA) came to after reviewing all of the available information. The same can be said of alcohol and tobacco—both legal drugs (and currently outside of the FDA's jurisdiction). How could anyone argue that adding a third substance to that mix is going to be beneficial?

- Alcohol and tobacco have proven harmful, addictive, and difficult to regulate. Alcohol is the third leading cause of death in the United States—each year over 100,000 Americans die of alcohol-related causes. The Surgeon General estimates that problems resulting from alcohol use and abuse cost society almost $200 billion every year, and that these costs are far higher than any revenue generated by alcohol taxes.[2]

- Tobacco, the other substance that often is suggested as a model for 'legal' marijuana, offers a picture of a similarly bleak future. The Center for Disease Control estimates that the total economic costs associated with cigarette smoking is approximately $7.18 per pack of cigarettes sold in the United States. The revenue generated to cover these costs? The federal excise tax is $1.01 per pack of cigarettes.[3] The median state cigarette excise tax rate, as of January 1, 2007, is 80 cents.[4] This hardly sounds like an "economic windfall" that cures our budget woes.

- If we were to regulate marijuana, we would have to concede that it's acceptable for society to profit from a person's addiction. There were approximately 38,000 overdose deaths for illicit drugs and non-medical use of prescription drugs during 2006, according to the Center for Disease Control.[5] How much are those lives worth?

- The cost of treatment and rehabilitation from addiction and usage associated illnesses far outweighs the cost of any revenue possibly be generated; a government estimate of the cost of drug use just for one year (2002) was more than $180 billion. Regulation hasn't kept prescription drugs, alcohol, or tobacco from being abused. The excise taxes that are collected from these activities only cover a portion of the costs of their misuse.

- Studies demonstrate that when people perceive the use of drugs as harmless, drug use increases— if marijuana or other drugs were legalized, it is certain that the perceived harm would decrease, making the incidence of use rise, regardless of age-related regulations.

- Suggesting that the only costs, caused by the illegality of drugs are law enforcement costs ignores lives and livelihoods lost due to addiction and overdose. Lowering or eliminating the legal restrictions for drugs will result in increased availability, and greater use, with higher healthcare costs and increased criminal activity. We have seen these costs go up when other nations have gone down this path, and we should not make the same mistakes.

- For example, when The Netherlands liberalized their drug laws allowing the public sale of marijuana, they saw marijuana use among 18-25 years olds double, and the heroin addiction levels triple. They have since reversed this trend, and have begun implementing tighter drug controls. Indeed, today over 70 percent of Dutch municipalities have local zero-tolerance laws.[6] Similarly, when the United Kingdom relaxed their drug laws to allow physicians to prescribe heroin to certain classes of addicts, they saw an entirely new class of youthful users emerge. According to social scientist James Q. Wilson, the British Government's experiment with controlled heroin distribution resulted in a minimum of a 30-fold increase in the number of addicts in 10 years. *(See page 60 for more details on European legalization experiments.)*

- While the notion that each individual can make their own choices without affecting anyone is a nice theory, it is impractical in today's interconnected world. The health and social costs generated by addiction are borne not just by the drug user, but by everyone. The purpose of an effective drug policy should be to lessen the harm that illegal drugs do to our society. Lowering or eliminating the current legal and social restrictions that limit the availability and social acceptance of drug use would have the opposite result, both domestically and internationally.

- Some have hypothesized that there has already been a loss of state tax revenue because of actions taken against marijuana traffickers who purport to be operating in furtherance of state marijuana legalization laws. In fact, this is a question that some jurisdictions in California have raised directly with the Department of Justice. In summary, the Department of Justice replied that income derived from the sale of marijuana, whether in California or not, represents proceeds of illegal drug trafficking, and as such is forfeitable under federal law.

- The State of California is neither an innocent owner nor a lien holder in regards to collecting illegal drug proceeds.[7] All right, title, and interest in property subject to forfeiture under the Controlled Substance Act – including all money and other proceeds of illegal drug sales – shall vest in the United States upon commission of the illegal act giving rise to the forfeiture.[8] Under the supremacy clause of the United States Constitution, a state may not impose a sales tax, or any other tax, on the property of the United States.[9]

- Nonetheless, if a government entity wishes to assert a legal claim to any seized funds, the Civil Asset Forfeiture Reform Act of 2000 (CAFRA) provides a mechanism for it to do so, which begins by submitting a claim in a timely manner and in the appropriate legal proceeding. In evaluating whether to maintain a legal claim please consider that general creditors lack standing to contest the federal forfeiture of property.[10] Thus, if a state or local government asserts that it is a general creditor based upon unreported and/or unpaid sales taxes, it might look to those entities whose property was seized, rather than the federal government, for relief.

- If instead the state or local governments claim some specific interest in the seized funds – funds which were derived from the distribution of a controlled substance – then such an interest would have to be evaluated according to principles of federal forfeiture law.[11] To date, no state or local entity has made such claims.

3 "Drug laws infringe on state's rights."

- The federal government does not focus its marijuana enforcement resources on individual patients with cancer or other serious illnesses, and the Attorney General has directed that this remain the case.

- The Attorney General has determined that the Department of Justice will focus its investigation, enforcement, and prosecution efforts regarding the manufacture and distribution of marijuana on significant drug traffickers. Indicators of significant drug trafficking may include citizen complaints, use of firearms, violence, sales to minors, marketing, sales for profit, excessive amounts of cash, money laundering, excessive volumes of controlled substances, requests for federal assistance from local law enforcement, sale of other illegal drugs, or any other identified factor that would demonstrate that marijuana growers or distributors are trying to use state laws as a shield for illegal activity.

- Any change to the legal status of marijuana should be done through the mechanisms established by the Controlled Substances Act (CSA), which requires action by the Food and Drug Administration (FDA) and the DEA, or by Congress.

- The state's rights "argument" is most popular in discussions regarding "medical" marijuana ballot initiatives that have passed in 14 States. Marijuana remains a Schedule I controlled substance under the CSA.[12] This is consistent with the fact that the drug has never been approved by the FDA for marketing in the United States because scientific studies have never established that marijuana can be used safely and effectively for the treatment of any disease or condition.[13] Marijuana's placement in Schedule I of the CSA results in the following legal consequences: marijuana may not be dispensed for medical use in the United States; it is illegal to manufacture, distribute, or possess marijuana for any purpose (other than government-approved research); and there is no "medical necessity" defense to the CSA prohibitions relating to marijuana.[14]

- The Supreme Court's decisions in *United States v. Oakland Cannabis Buyers' Cooperative (OCBC)*[15] and *Gonzales v. Raich*[16] make clear, regardless of whether one complies with the California marijuana legalization law, it remains illegal under the CSA for any person to cultivate, distribute, or possess marijuana for claimed "medical reasons."

- The United States has also signed various international treaties to control illegal drug activity.[17] The International Narcotics Control Board (INCB) of the United Nations is charged with monitoring compliance with the drug control treaties. The INCB pointed out that the state marijuana initiatives recently passed in the United States are contrary to United States federal law. The report called on the United States to "vigorously enforce its federal law" in the face of these initiatives. The report further stated: "The decision of whether a substance should be authorized for medical use has always been taken, and should continue to be taken, in all countries by the bodies designated to regulate and register medicines. Such decisions should have a sound medical and scientific basis and should not be made in accordance with referendums organized by interest groups."[18]

- The authority of the DEA to investigate those growing, selling, or possessing marijuana, irrespective of state law, has been reaffirmed by recent rulings by the United States Supreme Court. In rejecting the notion that marijuana activities purportedly taking place in compliance with California law and supposedly on a "wholly intrastate" basis are beyond the reach of Congress' commerce clause authority, the Supreme Court stated in *Raich*:

    The CSA designates marijuana as contraband for *any* purpose; in fact, by characterizing marijuana as a Schedule I drug, Congress expressly found that the drug has no acceptable medical uses. Moreover, the CSA is a comprehensive regulatory regime specifically designed to regulate which controlled substances can be utilized for medicinal purposes, and in what manner... Thus, even if respondents were correct that marijuana does have accepted medical uses and thus should be re-designated as a lesser schedule drug, the CSA would still impose controls beyond what is required by California law. The CSA requires manufacturers, physicians, pharmacies, and other handlers of controlled substances to comply with statutory and regulatory provisions mandating registration with the DEA; compliance with specific production quotas; security controls to guard against diversion; record keeping and reporting obligations, and prescription requirements. Furthermore, the dispensing of new drugs, even when doctors approve their use, must await federal approval.[19]

The Court also provided the following explanation for rejecting the marijuana trafficker's commerce clause argument in *Raich*:

> Given the enforcement difficulties that attend distinguishing between marijuana cultivated locally and marijuana grown elsewhere, and concerns about diversion into illicit channels, we have no difficulty concluding that Congress had a rational basis for believing that failure to regulate the intrastate manufacture and possession of marijuana would leave a gaping hole in the CSA.[20]

- In addition, the Supreme Court's decision in *OCBC* makes clear that the marijuana activities of a California "cannabis club" are illegal under the CSA. The Supreme Court rulings indicate unequivocally that the CSA prohibitions on manufacturing, distributing, and possessing marijuana apply regardless of whether the person engaging in such activity claims to have a "medical necessity," claims to be acting in accordance with state law, or claims to be acting in a wholly intrastate manner.

- The DEA is responsible for enforcing the CSA. Accordingly, DEA is obligated to take all appropriate law enforcement actions, use all of the tools at our disposal, and to investigate any organization, including marijuana distribution facilities (sometimes referred to by their operators as "cannabis clubs") that are engaged in the unlawful manufacture and distribution of controlled substances.

- Some have hypothesized that there has already been a loss of state tax revenue because of actions taken against marijuana "dispensaries." In fact, this is a question that some jurisdictions in California have raised directly with the Department of Justice. In summary, the Department replied that income derived from the sale of marijuana, whether in California or not, represents proceeds of illegal drug trafficking, and as such is forfeitable under federal law.

- The State of California is neither an innocent owner nor a lien holder in regards to collecting illegal drug proceeds.[21] All right, title, and interest in property subject to forfeiture under the CSA – including all money and other proceeds of illegal drug sales – shall vest to the United States upon commission of the illegal act giving rise to the forfeiture.[22] Under the supremacy clause of the United States Constitution, a state may not impose a sales tax, or any other tax, on the property of the United States.[23]

- Nonetheless, if a state entity wishes to assert a legal claim to any seized funds, CAFRA provides a mechanism for it to do so, which begins by submitting a claim in a timely manner and in the appropriate legal proceeding. In evaluating whether to maintain a legal claim please consider that general creditors lack standing to contest the federal forfeiture of property.[24] Thus, if a state or local entity asserts that it is a general creditor based upon unreported and/or unpaid sales taxes, it might look to those entities whose property was seized, rather than the federal government, for relief.

4 "Prohibition didn't work in the 20's and it doesn't work now."

- Claims that prohibition didn't work overlook the fact that most historians agree that national prohibition succeeded both in lowering consumption and in retaining political support until the great depression radically changed voters' priorities. Repeal resulted more from this contextual shift than from characteristics of prohibition itself.

- One favorite argument of those who claim prohibition didn't work point to the growth of organized crime. Although organized crime flourished under its sway, historians trace the beginnings of organized crime in the United States to the mid to late-1800s. Organized crime existed before prohibition was enacted, and persists long after its repeal.

- The laws and enforcement mechanisms created after 1919 by the 18th Amendment and the Volstead Act, which charged the Treasury Department with enforcement of the new restrictions, was far from all-embracing. The amendment prohibited the commercial manufacture and distribution of alcoholic beverages; it did not prohibit use, nor production for one's own consumption.

- Alcohol consumption declined dramatically during prohibition. Cirrhosis death rates for men were 29.5 per 100,000 in 1911 and 10.7 in 1929. Admissions to State mental hospitals for alcoholic psychosis declined from 10.1 per 100,000 in 1919 to 4.7 in 1928.

- Arrests for public drunkenness and disorderly conduct declined 50 percent between 1916 and 1922. For the population as a whole, the best estimates are that consumption of alcohol declined by 30 percent to 50 percent. Violent crime did not increase dramatically during prohibition. Homicide rates rose dramatically from 1900 to 1910 but remained roughly constant during prohibition's 14 year rule.[26] Organized crime may have become more visible and lurid during prohibition, but it existed before and after.

- Following the repeal of prohibition, alcohol consumption increased. Prohibition did not end alcohol use, but it did succeed in reducing, by one-third, the consumption of a product that had wide historical and popular sanction.

- The parallel between alcohol prohibition in the 1920's and the current status of marijuana, heroin, and other dangerous drugs is tenuous. The 18th Amendment took a popular activity, alcohol sales, which was widely tolerated, and made it illegal. It did so after more than a century of growing concern over the effects of excessive alcohol consumption was having on society. In contrast, the use of marijuana, heroin, or other controlled drugs has never been a widely accepted activity.

- In addition, the idealistic goals of prohibition went beyond what many initial supporters of prohibition thought they were supporting, and lacked flexibility that would allow policy adjustments to changes in the facts surrounding alcohol. In contrast, our nation's current drug laws are built upon the Controlled Substances Act, which contains a series of increasingly restrictive schedules that allow for the appropriate regulation of various drugs, as well as a mechanism to move substances from one regulatory status to another should new information about the use of a controlled substance be established.

- Not only are the facts of prohibition misunderstood, but the lessons are misapplied to marijuana legalization. The real lesson of prohibition is that the society can, indeed, make a dent in consumption through laws. There is a price to be paid for such restrictions, of course. But for drugs such as heroin and cocaine, which are dangerous but currently largely unpopular, that price is small relative to the benefits.

5 "Through drug laws Congress is attempting to legislate morality."

- John Adams, who helped draft the Constitution and later became our second president, declared, "Our Constitution was made only for a moral and religious people. It is wholly inadequate to govern of any other." This means that any and all just laws must be based on moral considerations. Our elected representatives are therefore bound to *legislate morality*.

- Morality is about right and wrong, and that's what laws put into legal form. All laws legislate morality (even speed limits imply a moral moral judgement). Everyone in politics — conservatives, libertarians and liberals — is trying in some degree to legislate morality. The complaint then, is not whether or not Congress is attempting to legislate morality, but whose morality is Congress attempting to legislate?

- The expectation that Congress will make these moral judgments comes from the Constitution, which decreed that a majority of the citizens, through the representatives elected to do our bidding, were given the right, the duty and responsibility, to make laws that would ensure domestic tranquility, defend our borders, and promote a safe and wholesome environment for us all. These are all moral judgments.

- The Constitution also lays out the structure by which these moral judgments will be made. The principal of majority rule, the balance of power between the president, the; judiciary; and the Congress, and even the bi-cameral structure of Congress all work to provide an effective mechanism to legislate morality that is consistent with the desires—and therefore we must assume the morals—of a majority of Americans.

Notes

1. "National Drug Threat Assessment," December 2009, page III.
2. Marin Institute Fact Sheet, "The Costs of Alcohol," June 24, 2008.
3. As of April 1, 2009.
4. See: http://www.CDC.gov/tobacco.
5. Heron, et al, "Deaths: Final Data for 2006," U.S. Dept of Health and Human Services, Centers for Disease Control and Prevention, National Vital Statistics Reports, Vol. 57, Number 14, April 2009, DHHS Pub No (PAS) 2009-1120 (Tables 21 and 22), see: http://www.cdc.gov/nchs/data/nvsr/nvsr57/nvsr57_14.pdf.
6. INTRAVAL Bureau for Research and Consistency, "Coffeeshops in the Netherlands 2004," Dutch Ministry of Justice, June 2005, http://www.intraval.nl/en/b/b45_html.
7. See: 21 U.S.C. § 881.
8. 21 U.S.C. § 811(h).
9. See: McCullough v. Maryland, 17 U.S. 316 (1819); see also U.S. v. Cal. State Bd. of Equalization, 650 F.2d 1127 (9th Cir. 1981), 456 U.S. 901 (1982), aff'd, 456 U.S. 985 (1982), reh'g denied.
10. See, e g.: U.S. v. $20,193.39 U.S. Currency, 16 F.3d 344, 346 (9th Cir. 1994).
11. See, e.g.: 18 U.S.C. § 983(d)(3) and 21 U.S.C. § 853(n)(6)(B).
12. 21 U.S.C. § 812(c), Schedule I(c)(10).
13. See 66 Fed. Reg. 20038, 20050-52 (2001) (DEA denial of petition to remove marijuana from schedule I based on FDA scientific and medical evaluation), pet. for review dismissed, Gettman v. DEA, 290 F.3d 430 (D.C. Cir. 2002).
14. U.S. v. Oakland Cannabis Buyers' Cooperative 532 U.S. 483, 491, 494 & n.7 (2001).
15. 532 U.S. 483 (2001).
16. Gonzales v. Raich, 545 U.S. 1 (2005).
17. The main drug control treaties currently in force to which the United States is signatory are: The Single Convention on Narcotic Drugs, 1961, 18 U.S.T. 1407; The Convention on Psychotropic Substances, 1971, 32 U.S.T. 543; and the Convention Against Illicit Traffic in Narcotic Drugs and Psychotropic Substances, 1988, 28 I.L.M. 493. Among the United States obligations pursuant to these treaties are: (i) To enact and carry out legislation disallowing the use of Schedule I drugs outside of authorized research; (ii) To make it a criminal offense, subject to imprisonment, to traffic in illicit drugs or to aid and abet such trafficking; and (iii) To prohibit the cultivation of marijuana except by persons licensed by, and under the direct supervision of, the federal Government.
18. U.N. International Narcotics Control Board, United Nations, "Report 1998" at par. 259, U.N. Sales No. E.99.XI.1, http://www.incb.org/incb/en/annual_report_1998.html.
19. 545 U.S. at 27-28.
20. 545 U.S. at 22
21. See 21 U.S.C. § 881.
22. 21 U.S.C. § 811(h).
23. See: McCullough v. Maryland, 17 U.S. 316 (1819); see also U.S. v. Cal. State Bd. of Equalization, 650 F.2d 1127 (9th Cir. 1981), 456 U.S. 901 (1982), affirmed, 456 U.S. 985 (1982), registration denied.
24. See, e g., U.S. v. $20,193.39 U.S. Currency, 16 F.3d 344, 346 (9th Cir. 1994).
25. See, e.g., 18 U.S.C. § 983(d)(3) and 21 U.S.C. § 853(n)(6)(B).
26. Moore, Mark H., "Actually, Prohibition Was a Success," Harvard's Kennedy School of Government, October 16, 1989.

(End notes continued on page 65)

13

Summary of the TOP 10 FACTS On Legalization

Fact 1: *Significant progress has been made in fighting drug use and drug trafficking in America.*

Legalization advocates claim that the fight against drugs has not been won and is, in fact, unwinnable. They frequently state that people still take drugs, drugs are widely available, and that efforts to change this are futile. They contend that legalization is the only workable alternative. The facts are contrary to such pessimism.

Fact 2: *A balanced approach of prevention, enforcement, and treatment are the keys in the fight against drug abuse.*

A successful drug policy must apply a balanced approach of prevention, enforcement, and treatment. All three aspects are crucial. For those who end up hooked on drugs, there are innovative programs, like drug courts, that offer non-violent users the option of seeking treatment.

Fact 3: *Drug use is regulated and access to drugs is controlled because drugs can be harmful.*

There is a popular misconception that some illegal drugs can be taken safely, with many advocates of legalization going so far as to suggest it can serve as medicine to heal anything from headaches to bipolar diseases. Many of today's drug dealers are savvy businessmen, and know how to capitalize on declining perceptions of risk associated with drug use.

Fact 4: *Smoked marijuana has never been and will never be scientifically approved medicine.*

According to the Institute of Medicine, there is no future for smoked marijuana as medicine. However, the prescription drug Marinol—a legal and safe version of medical marijuana which isolates the active ingredient of THC—has been studied and approved by the Food and Drug Administration as safe medicine when used as prescirbed. The difference between Marinol and marijuana is that you have to get a prescription for Marinol from a licensed physician—you can't buy it on a street corner, and you don't smoke it.

Fact 5: *Drug control spending is a minor portion of the U.S. budget. Compared to the social costs of drug abuse and addiction, government spending on drug control is minimal.*

Legalization advocates claim that the United States has wasted billions of dollars in its anti-drug efforts. But for those saved from drug addiction, these are not wasted dollars. Moreover, our fight against drug abuse and addiction is an ongoing struggle that should be treated like any other social problem. Would we give up on education or poverty simply because we haven't eliminated all the problems we have with them?

Fact 6: *Legalization of drugs will lead to increased use and increased levels of addiction.*

Legalization proponents claim that making illegal drugs legal would not cause more of these substances to be consumed, nor would addiction increase. They claim that many people can use drugs in moderation and that many would choose not to use drugs, just as many abstain from alcohol and tobacco now. Yet how much misery can already be attributed to alcoholism and smoking?

Fact 7: *Crime, violence, and drug use go hand-in-hand.*

Six times as many homicides are committed by people under the influence of drugs than by those who are looking for money to buy drugs. Most drug crimes aren't committed by people trying to pay for drugs; they're committed by people on drugs.

Fact 8: *Alcohol and tobacco have caused significant health, social, and crime problems, and legalized drugs would only make the situation worse.*

The "legalization lobby" claims drugs are no more dangerous than alcohol, no more harmful than smoking cigarettes. But drunk driving is one of the primary killers of Americans. Do we want our bus drivers, nurses, and airline pilots to be able to take drugs one evening, and operate freely at work the next day? Do we want to make "drugged" driving another primary killer?

Fact 9: *Europe's more liberal drug policies are not the right model for America.*

The "legalization lobby" claims that the "European model" of the drug problem is successful. However, since legalization of marijuana in the Netherlands, heroin addiction levels have tripled. Their "Needle Park" is a poor model for America.

Fact 10: *Most non-violent drug users get treatment, not jail time.*

There is a popular myth that America's prisons are filling up with drug users arrested for simple possession of marijuana. This is a myth. In reality, a vast majority of inmates in state and federal prison for marijuana have been found guilty of much more than simple possession, and many of those serving time for marijuana possession pled down to possession in order to avoid prosecution on more serious charges.

Fact 1: Significant progress has been made in fighting drug use and drug trafficking in America.

Legalization advocates claim that the fight against drugs has not been won and is, in fact, unconquerable. They frequently state that people still take drugs, drugs are widely available, and that efforts to change this are futile. They contend that legalization is the only workable alternative.

The facts are contrary to such pessimism:

Demand Reduction

- On the demand side, the U.S. has reduced casual use chronic use addiction to drugs, and prevented others from even starting to use them. According to the Monitoring the Future National Survey, between 2001 and 2008 illicit drug use was down 25 percent among 8th, 10th, and 12th grade students. That means approximately 900,000 fewer young people are using drugs today, compared to 2001. Marijuana use has fallen by 25 percent and youth use of drugs such as MDMA/Ecstasy, LSD, and methamphetamine have decreased by more than 50 percent.[27]

- The 2009 Monitoring the Future Survey reinforces the trends exhibited in 2008, and shows that the proportion of students reporting use of illicit drug other than marijuana has been gradually declining. The majority of illicit drugs covered in the study has remained the same compared with 2008, though most are at levels considerably below the level of the mid-1990s."[28]

- Current workforce drug testing data from Quest Diagnostics found that cocaine and methamphetamine use among U.S. job applicants and workers in the general workforce dropped significantly. Positive tests for cocaine declined by 38 percent from June 2006 to June 2008. Methamphetamine positive tests dropped almost 50 percent between 2005 and 2007. Overall drug use among workers subject to drug testing remains at the lowest level in the last 20 years.[29]

- The crack cocaine epidemic of the 1980s and early 1990s has diminished greatly in scope, and we've reduced the number of chronic heroin users over the last decade. In addition, the number of new marijuana users and cocaine users continues to steadily decrease.

- Yet there is still much progress to be made. There are still far too many people using cocaine, heroin, and other illegal drugs. In addition, there are emerging drug threats like the non-medical use of prescription pain relievers and over-the-counter cough medicine. But the fact is that our current policies balancing prevention, enforcement, and treatment have kept drug usage outside the scope of acceptable behavior.

Supply Reduction

- There have been many successes on the supply side of the drug fight as well. For example, purity levels of Colombian cocaine are declining, according to an analysis of samples seized from traffickers and bought from street dealers in the United States. The average purity of cocaine has declined from 86 percent in 1998, to 44 percent in 2008. At the same time, the price of one gram of cocaine rose 104.5 percent from $97.62 to $199.60. There are a number of possible reasons for this decline in purity, including DEA supply reduction efforts in South America.[31]

- The British Serious Organized Crime Agency (SOCA) reports a similar trend. The price per kilo of cocaine has risen from £36,000 per kilo in the summer of 2008 to £45,000 per kilo in March 2009. In addition, SOCA reported that the purity levels of street sales of cocaine have been reduced significantly since the summer of 2008, meaning purchasers were often paying four or five times extra for the actual cocaine purchased.[32]

- DEA has been very active with international efforts targeting precursor chemicals, such as the International Narcotics Control Board (INCB) *Projects Prism* and *Cohesion*, which have led to major precursor seizures and the general development of precursor chemical awareness across the globe. *Project Prism* is a global initiative focusing on the illicit trade of methamphetamine precursor chemicals and *Project Cohesion* focuses on the illicit trade of precursor chemicals used to manufacture heroin and cocaine.

  For instance, between January 2007 and September 2008, the *Project Prism* Operations *Crystal Flow (2007)* and *Ice Block (2008)* allowed international authorities to share intelligence and prevent an estimated 100 tons of methamphetamine precursor chemicals from being diverted to the illicit market.

- The combined effects of all these measures have disrupted illicit drug production and have caused black market prices of precursor chemicals to rise drastically.

- U.S. border initiatives are having a major impact on the activities of Mexican drug trafficking organizations. Excellent cooperation between the U.S. and Mexican governments has resulted in the extradition of major traffickers to the U.S. for prosecution; joint operations to stem the flow of drugs, chemicals and money across the Southwest border; and the targeting of major drug cartels and border "gatekeepers."

- For example, this cooperation has also resulted in increased import restrictions of ephedrine and pseudoephedrine in Mexico, helping to decrease methamphetamine production and reduce the flow of methamphetamine from Mexico into the United States.

- According to data collected by the El Paso Intelligence Center, methamphetamine seizures along the Southwest border increased by 91 percent from 1,170 kilograms in 2001 to 2,232 kilograms in 2008.

- Trafficking organizations that sell drugs are finding that their profession has become a lot more costly worldwide. For example in the mid-1990s, the DEA helped dismantle Burma's Shan United Army, at the time the world's largest heroin trafficking organization. In two years this operation helped reduce the amount of Southeast Asian heroin in the United States from 63 percent of the market to 17 percent of the market. In the mid-1990s, the DEA helped disrupt the Cali Cartel, which had been responsible for much of the world's cocaine.

- Progress does not come overnight. America has had a long, dark struggle with drugs. It's not a war we've been fighting for 20 years—we've been fighting it for *120 years*. In 1880, many drugs, including opium and cocaine, were legal. We didn't know the harm they caused, but we soon learned. We saw the highest level of drug use ever in our nation, per capita. There were over 400,000 opium addicts in our nation. That's twice as many addicts and users per capita as there are today. Like today, we saw rising crime that accompanied drug abuse. But we fought those problems by passing and enforcing tough laws and by educating the public about the dangers of these drugs. This vigilance worked: by World War II, drug use was reduced to the very margins of society, and that's just where we want to keep it.

- A successful drug policy must apply a balanced approach of prevention, enforcement, and treatment. All three aspects are crucial. For those who end up hooked on drugs, there are innovative programs, like drug courts, that offer non-violent users the option of seeking treatment.

Fact 2: A balanced approach of prevention, enforcement, and treatment are the keys in the fight against drug abuse.

- The 2010 National Drug Control Strategy Report highlights three national priorities: stopping drug initiation; reducing drug abuse and addiction; and disrupting the market for illegal drugs.[34]

- In 2008, according to the National Survey on Drug Use and Health, an estimated 20.1 million Americans aged 12 or older were current (past month) illicit drug users, meaning they had used an illicit drug during the month prior to the survey interview. This estimate represents 8 percent of the population aged 12 years old or older. Illicit drugs include marijuana/hashish, cocaine (including crack), heroin, hallucinogens, inhalants, or prescription-type psychotherapeutics used non-medically. [35]

- Over the years, some people have advocated a policy that focuses narrowly on controlling the supply of drugs. Others have said that society should rely on treatment alone. Still others say that prevention is the only viable solution. These are outdated approaches to a modern, effective strategy. Today, there is general agreement that we must integrate all three aspects in a balanced strategy if we are to continue to make progress.

Stopping Drug Initiation

- No one starts life wanting to be a drug addict. We must teach our children about the dangers and consequences of drug use, teach them what to do when they are offered drugs, and keep re-enforcing these lessons. Research has shown that if a child can reach adulthood without ever having tried drugs, the chances of him ever being addicted are significantly less.[37]

- The 2010 National Drug Control Strategy lays out a comprehensive support to prevention programs, including building on community level activities, targeted substance abuse prevention programs in schools and institutions of higher learning, in the workplace, on the roads, in the military, and on the playing fields. This comprehensive approach means educating the public about the dangers of drug use, as well as working with medical and pharmaceutical organizations to prevent the diversion of prescription drugs.[38]

Reducing Drug Abuse and Addiction

- Substance abuse treatment costs our nation over one half-trillion dollars annually, and treatment can help reduce these costs by far more than the expense of that treatment.[39]

- Conservatively, every $1 invested in addiction treatment programs yields a return of between $4 and $7 in reduced drug-related crime, criminal justice costs, and theft. When savings related to health care are included, total savings can rise to $12 for every $1 invested.

Drug Courts

- For those who end up hooked on drugs there are also programs, like drug courts, that offer non-violent users the option of seeking treatment. Drug courts provide court supervision, unlike voluntary treatment centers. Drug courts are a good example of a balanced approach to fighting drug abuse and addiction in our country. These courts are given a special responsibility to handle cases involving drug-addicted offenders through an extensive supervision and treatment program. Drug court programs use the varied experiences and skills of a wide variety of law enforcement and treatment professionals: judges, prosecutors, defense counsel, substance abuse treatment specialists, probation officers, law enforcement and correctional personnel, educational and vocational experts, community leaders and others — all focused on one goal: to help cure addicts of their addiction, and keep them cured.

- Nationwide, 75 percent of drug court graduates remain arrest-free at least two years after leaving the program.[40]

- A 2000 Vera Institute of Justice report concluded that "the body of literature on recidivism is now strong enough that despite lingering methodological weaknesses, to conclude that completing a drug court program reduces the likelihood of future arrest." [41]

- The largest statewide study on drug courts to date was released in 2003 by the Center for Court Innovation (CCI). The study analyzed the impact of the New York State drug court system. The study found that the re-conviction rate among 2,135 defendants who participated in six of the state's drug courts was, on average, significantly lower (13 percent to 47 percent) over three years than the for the same types of offenders who did not enter the drug court. The study also concluded that drug court cases reached initial disposition more quickly than conventional court cases, and that the statewide drug court retention rate was approximately 65 percent, exceeding the national average of 60 percent.[42]

- Nonviolent drug offenders in drug courts in St. Louis, Missouri, who were placed in treatment instead of prison generally earned more money and took less from the welfare system than those who successfully completed probation. The study compared the 219 individuals who were the program's first graduates in 2001 with 219 people who pleaded guilty to drug charges during the same period and completed probation. For each drug court graduate, the cost to taxpayers was $7,793, which was $1,449 more than those on probation. However, during the two years following program completion, each graduate cost the city $2,615 less than those on probation. These savings were realized in higher wages and related taxes paid, as well as lower costs for health care and mental health services.[43]

- Drug courts save taxpayers money. The Urban Institute estimates a favorable cost/benefit ratio as high as $3.36 for every $1.00 invested in treating drug-addicted offenders in drug courts.[44]

Risk Perception

- The perception of risk also plays an important part in whether kids abuse drugs and other substances. Researchers from the UIC ImpacTeen Project and University of Michigan Youth Education and Society Project (YES!) reported in 2000 that marijuana use among youth decreased as marijuana prices and perceived harmfulness rose. Their study also assessed the extent to which trends in marijuana prices and perceptions of use risks predict cycles in youth marijuana use. Their research noted that use of marijuana among high school seniors declined to a recorded low between 1981 and 1992, when price more than tripled. The trend reversed itself after 1992, when price fell by 16 percent. The study shows that perceived risk of harm from marijuana use had a substantial impact on the reduction in marijuana use between 1981 and 1992 (as perceived risk rose) and in the subsequent increase in use after 1992 (as perceived risk declined).[45] These conclusions are consistent with ones reached earlier by the University of Michigan investigators, who for years have argued the importance of perceived risk in explaining trends in the use of various drugs.

Enforcing Drug Laws

- Enforcement of our laws creates risks that discourage drug use. Laws which clearly define what is legal and illegal and send a strong signal to young and old alike what the boundaries are.

- Law enforcement plays an important role in the drug court program. It is especially important in the beginning of the process because it often triggers treatment for people who need it. Most people do not volunteer for drug treatment. It is more often an outside motivator, like an arrest, that gets —and keeps— people in treatment. If treatment fails it is important for judges to keep people incarcerated.

- Price and availability can also affect the choice of whether to abuse drugs. Strong drug enforcement affects the price and purity of drugs and impacts demand. A study released in 2005, *Marijuana Use and Policy: What We Know and Have Yet To Learn,* by Rosalie Liccardo Pacula found that price matters, and marijuana prevalence rates are responsive to changes in perceived risk.[47]

- In addition, even though the number of marijuana primary diagnoses was significantly lower than those for alcohol, heroin, and cocaine, the mean length of stay for marijuana episodes was three times longer than for alcohol and heroin discharges, and more than two times longer than for cocaine diagnoses with the mean charge per marijuana discharge was nearly twice as large as those for any of the other substances.

- According to DEA's System to Retrieve Information on Drug Evidence (STRIDE) database, the average price per pure gram of methamphetamine increased 73 percent from January 2007 through September 2008, from $141.42 to $244.53. During the same period, the purity of meth dropped 31 percent. From January 2007 through September 2007, there was a 44 percent increase in the average price per pure gram of cocaine in the United States (from $95.35 to $136.93), and there was a corresponding 15 percent decrease in cocaine purity in the illegal drug market in the United States.

- These findings support earlier indicators of reductions in cocaine availability in 37 American cities, based on law enforcement intelligence reports and unprecedented reductions in the number of employees testing positive for cocaine in workplace drug tests.

- The National Survey on Drug Use and Health estimated the number of past month methamphetamine users declined by over half between 2006, and 2008. The numbers were 731,000 in 2006, 529,000 in 2007, and 314,000 in 2008. It also reported an estimated 2.1 million people aged 12 or older who used cocaine in the past month in 2008 versus 2.4 million 2006, and a significant decline in crack users from 702,000 in 2006 to 359,000 in 2008.[48]

Fact 3: Drug use is regulated, and access to drugs is controlled, because drugs can be harmful.

- There is a popular misconception that some illegal drugs can be taken safely, with many advocates of legalization going so far as to suggest it can serve as medicine to heal anything from headaches to bipolar diseases. Many of today's drug dealers are savvy businessmen, and know how to capitalize on declining perceptions of risk associated with drug use.

- Marijuana is sold in California by some traffikers as a food product, including as an ingredient in baked goods, soda, liquids, peanut butter, cereal, soup, and ice cream. The food products are typically labeled, "3X," "6X," "9X" and "10x," which describes its THC potency. There are no standards at all for these products: they are not inspected by anyone prior to selling them; there are no expiration dates; no list of ingredients, and no danger warnings on packaging. Some of these marijuana food and beverage products have been packaged in wrappers and labels made to purposely resemble legitimate food items.[49]

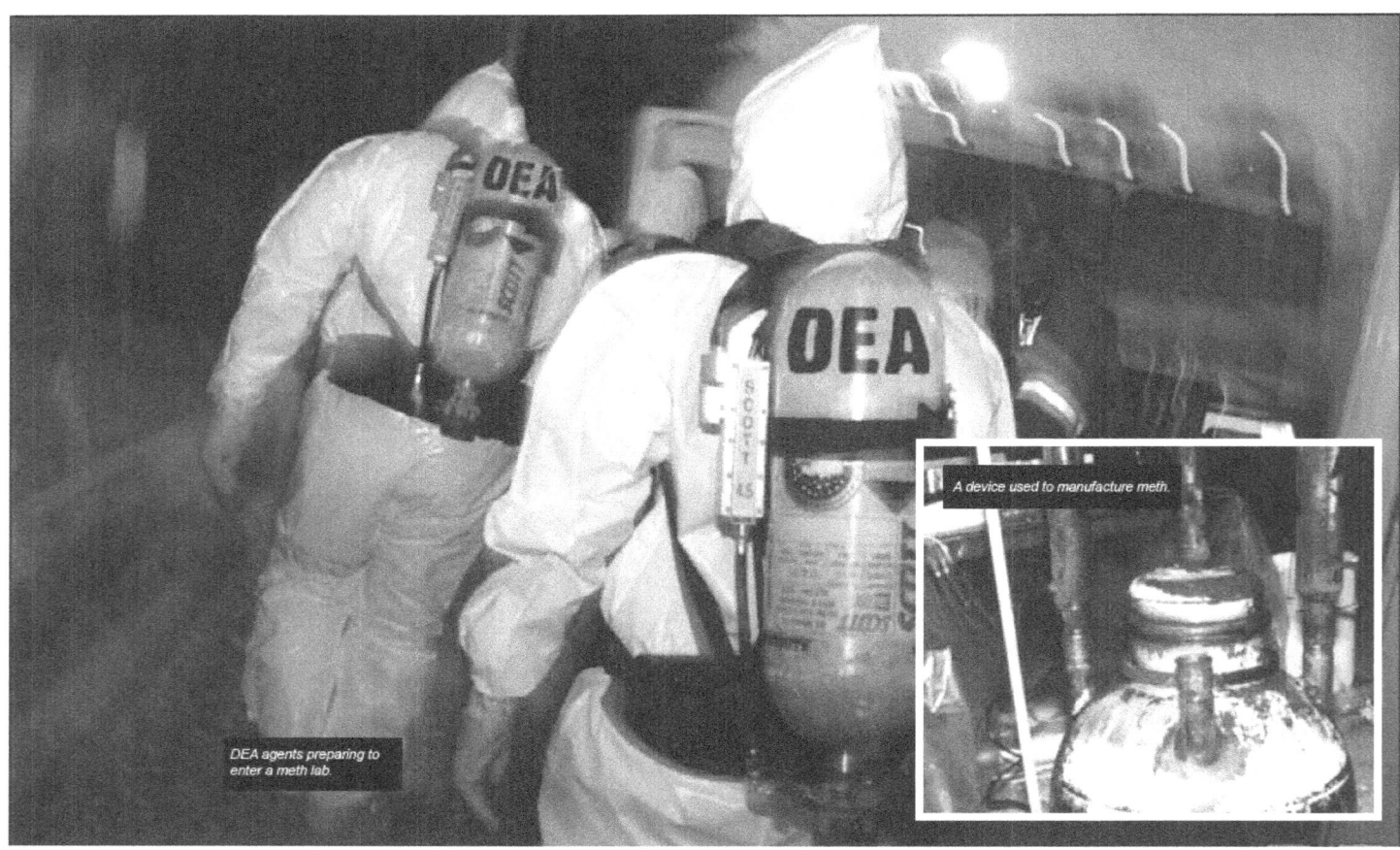

DEA agents preparing to enter a meth lab.

A device used to manufacture meth.

- Marijuana traffickers often advertise recommendations for "medical" marijuana or your money back.[50] In 2006 in Los Angeles, a Van Nuys area patrol officer was dispatched to Grant High School to investigate an assault. While walking across campus, the officer observed a card placed on several vehicles in the school parking lot that advertised medical marijuana recommendations at JT Medical Group, Inc., in North Hollywood (approximately 1/2 mile from the school). The card stated, "Yes, in the State of California, it is still legal to own, grow, and smoke medical marijuana as long as you do it properly. Qualifying is simple and our experienced physicians are more than happy to help you." The card also stated, "If you do not qualify for a recommendation your visit is free."

> *By 2004, drug poisonings accounted for 19,838 deaths, or 94.7 percent of all unintentional poisioning deaths.*

- Drug dealers create marijuana and cocaine products sold as candy.[51] They created "cheese" in the Dallas area by mixing acetaminophen, diphenhydramine hydrochloride, and up to 8 percent heroin.[52] They imprint Ecstasy pills with cartoon characters and designer logos.

- Because of the new marketing tactics of drug promoters, and an increasing drumbeat from those seeking to legalize drugs, attitudes towards drugs are softening. Attitudes toward substance abuse, often seen as harbingers of change in use rates, began turning upward in 2009. "The 2009 Monitoring the Futrue Survey is a warning sign, and the continued erosion in youth attitudes and behavior toward substance abuse should give pause to all parents and policymakers," said Director Gil Kerlikowske, of the White House Office of National Drug Control Policy. "Considering the troublesome data from national and local surveys, this latest data confirms that we must redouble our efforts to implement a comprehensive, evidenced-based approach to preventing and treating drug use."[53]

- Use of illegal drugs has deadly consequences. According to a report in the February 9, 2007 Morbidity and Mortality Weekly Report, "In 2004, poisoning was second only to motor-vehicle crashes as a cause of death from unintentional injury in the United States. Nearly all poisoning deaths in the United States are attributed to drugs, and most drug poisonings result from the abuse of prescription and illegal drugs."[54]

- To further examine this trend, Centers for Disease Control analyzed current data from the National Vital Statistics System. The report determined that poisoning mortality rates in the United States increased each year from 1999 to 2004, rising 62.5 percent during the five-year period. The increase in deaths due to unintentional poisoning occurred almost exclusively among those whose deaths were attributed to unintentional drug poisoning. By 2004, drug poisoning accounted for 19,838 deaths, or 94.7 percent of all unintentional poisoning deaths.[55]

- Drug use is deadly—far deadlier than alcohol. In 2006, 38,396 persons died of drug-induced causes in the United States. By comparison, there were 22,073 deaths due to alcohol-induced causes.[56] This means deaths caused by drug use are almost 174 percent higher than those due to alcohol.

- During this same timeframe, an estimated 20.4 million Americans aged 12 or older (8.3 percent of the population) were current (past month) illicit drug users, meaning they had used an illicit drug during the month. By comparison, an estimated 125 million Americans aged 12 or older (50.9 percent) were current (past month) drinkers, meaning they had at least one drink during the last 30 days. Even if you only consider the 23 percent of individuals who reported binge drinking in the last month, you are still looking at more than one-fifth of Americans (57 million people) aged 12 or older, a significantly larger user population than those reporting using illicit drugs. This means that approximately six times as many Americans use alcohol than illicit drugs. More people die from drug-related causes than alcohol, but more people consume alcohol than drugs.[57]

Cocaine

- Cocaine is a powerfully addictive stimulant that directly affects the brain. Cocaine is not a new drug — in fact, it is one of the oldest known drugs. The pure chemical, cocaine hydrochloride, has been an abused substance for more than 100 years, and coca leaves, the source of cocaine, have been ingested for thousands of years.[58]

- Cocaine abuse has a long history and is rooted into the drug culture in the United States. It is an intense euphoric drug with strong addictive potential. With the increase in purity, the advent of the free-base form of the cocaine ("crack"), and its all too easy availability on the street, cocaine continues to burden both the law enforcement and health care systems in America. [59]

- Cocaine's effects appear almost immediately after a single dose, and disappears within a few minutes or hours. Taken in small amounts (up to 100 mg), cocaine usually makes the user feel euphoric, energetic, talkative, and mentally alert, especially to the sensations of sight, sound, and touch. It can also temporarily decrease the need for food and sleep. Some users find that the drug helps them perform simple physical and intellectual tasks more quickly, while others experience the opposite effect.[60]

Solidified cocaine known as CRACK coaine

Cocaine in powdered form

- The short-term physiological effects of cocaine include constricted blood vessels; dilated pupils; and increased temperature, heart rate, and blood pressure. Large amounts (several hundred milligrams or more) intensify the user's high, but may also lead to bizarre, erratic, and violent behavior. These users may experience tremors, vertigo, muscle twitches, paranoia, or with repeated doses a toxic reaction closely resembling amphetamine poisoning. Some users of cocaine report feelings of restlessness, irritability, and anxiety. In rare instances, sudden death can occur on the first use of cocaine, or unexpectedly thereafter. Cocaine-related deaths are often a result of cardiac arrest or seizures followed by respiratory arrest.[61]

- Because cocaine is a powerfully addictive drug users may have difficulty predicting or controlling the extent to which they will continue to want or use the drug. Cocaine's stimulant and addictive effects are thought to be primarily a result of its ability to inhibit the re-absorption of dopamine by nerve cells. Dopamine is released as part of the brain's reward system, and is either directly or indirectly involved in the addictive properties of every major drug of abuse.[62]

- A significant tolerance to cocaine's high may develop, with many addicts reporting that they seek but fail to achieve as much pleasure as they did from their first experience. Some users will frequently increase their doses to intensify and prolong the euphoric effects. While tolerance to the high can occur, users can also become more sensitive to cocaine's anesthetic and convulsant effects, without increasing the dose taken. This increased sensitivity may explain some deaths occurring after apparently low doses of cocaine.[63]

- Use of cocaine in a binge, during which the drug is taken repeatedly and at increasingly high doses, leads to a state of increasing irritability, restlessness, and paranoia. This may result in a full-blown paranoid psychosis in which the individual loses touch with reality and experiences auditory hallucinations.[64]

- According to the 2008 National Survey on Drug Use and Health (NSDUH), an estimated 2.1 million people aged 12 or older used cocaine in the past month in 2008 versus 2.4 million in 2006. The number of past month crack users also declined significantly to 359,000 in 2008 vs. 702,000 in 2006.[65]

- The 2008 Monitoring the Future Survey found that trends in 30-day prevalence of cocaine use among 8th, 10th, and 12th graders has shown a marked decrease from 2006. Reported cocaine use by 8th graders decreased from 1 percent to 0.8 percent, by 10th graders from 1.5 percent to 0.9 percent, and for 12th graders from 2.5 percent in 2006 to 1.3 percent in 2008. [66]

- According to 2006 Drug Abuse Warning Network (DAWN) data released in August 2008, cocaine is the most frequently reported illegal drug in hospital emergency department visits, accounting for close to 1 in 3 (31 percent) of drug related emergency room visits.[67]

Heroin in a powdered form.

Black tar heroin.

Heroin

- Heroin is an illegal, highly addictive drug. It is both the most abused, and the most rapidly acting of opiates. Heroin is processed from morphine, a naturally occurring substance extracted from the seed pod of certain varieties of poppy plants. It is typically sold as a white or brownish powder, or as the black sticky substance known on the streets as "black tar heroin." Although purer heroin is becoming more common, most street heroin is "cut" with other drugs or with substances such as sugar, starch, powdered milk, or quinine. Street heroin can also be cut with strychnine, fentanyl, or other poisons. Because heroin abusers do not know the actual strength of the drug or its true contents, they are at risk of overdose or death. Heroin also poses special problems because of the transmission of HIV and other diseases that can occur from sharing needles or other injection equipment.[68]

- First synthesized from morphine in 1874, heroin was not extensively used in medicine until the early 1900s. Commercial production of the new pain remedy was first started in 1898. It initially received widespread acceptance from the medical profession, and physicians remained unaware of its addiction potential for years. The first comprehensive control of heroin occurred with the Harrison Narcotic Act of 1914. Today, heroin is an illicit substance having no medical utility in the United States.[69]

- Heroin can be injected, smoked, or sniffed/snorted. Injection is the most efficient way to administer low-purity heroin. The availability of high-purity heroin, however, and the fear of infection by sharing needles has made snorting and smoking the drug more common. National Institute on Drug Abuse (NIDA) researchers have confirmed that all forms of heroin administration are addictive.[70]

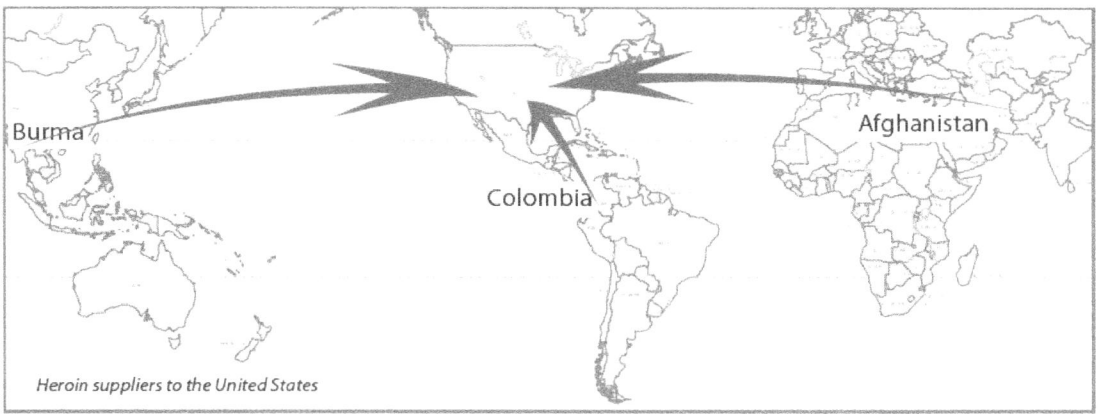

Heroin suppliers to the United States

- Chronic users may develop collapsed veins, infection of the heart lining and valves, abscesses, cellulites, and liver disease. Pulmonary complications, including various types of pneumonia, may result from the poor health condition of the abuser, as well as from heroin's depressing effects on respiration. In addition to the effects of the drug itself, street heroin may have additives that do not readily dissolve and result in clogging the blood vessels that lead to the lungs, liver, kidneys, or brain. This can cause infection or even death of small patches of cells in vital organs.[71]

- Addiction is one of the most significant effects of heroin use. With regular heroin use, tolerance to the drug develops. Once this happens, the abuser must use more heroin to achieve the same intensity or effect that they are seeking. As higher doses of the drug are used over time, physical dependence and addiction to the drug develops.[72]

- Withdrawal, which in regular abusers may occur as early as a few hours after the last dose, produces drug craving, restlessness, muscle and bone pain, insomnia, diarrhea and vomiting, cold flashes with goose bumps ("cold turkey"), kicking movements ("kicking the habit"), and other symptoms. Major withdrawal symptoms peak between 48 and 72 hours after the last dose, and subside after about a week. Sudden withdrawal by heavily dependent users who are in poor health is occasionally fatal.[73]

- The U.S. heroin market is supplied entirely from foreign sources. Heroin is produced and made available in the United States from four distinct geographical areas: South America (Colombia), Mexico, Southeast Asia (primarily Burma), and Southwest Asia (principally Afghanistan). Heroin remains one of the least used illegal drugs, with around one percent of the population having tried it.

- Within the United States, there are two distinct heroin markets:

  o East of the Mississippi River, highly pure white powder heroin from South America is the predominant type, entering the United States primarily through the Caribbean.

  o West of the Mississippi River, black tar heroin from Mexico is the predominant type, entering the United States through the Southwest border.

- From 2005 to 2008, heroin use in the general U.S. workforce has increased 34 percent, from 2.9 per thousand to 3.9 per thousand, according to the National General Workplace Drug Testing Index maintained by Quest Diagnostics.

- According to 2009 Monitoriing the Future survey data, estimated heroin use among high school seniors has decreased slightly, from 1.5 percent in 2007 to 1.2 percent in 2009.[74]

- According to the 2008 National Survey on Drug Use and Health, there were an estimated 114,000 persons aged 12 and older who used heroin for the first time within the past year. The number of heroin initiates has not significantly changed since 2002, when the estimated number was 117,000. [75]

- According to the Centers for Disease Control, the incidence of heroin-caused death has increased 11 percent, from one per million in 2004 to 1.1 per million in 2005.

- According to 2006 Drug Abuse Awareness Network data, the estimated number of heroin-driven emergency department visits declined from 214,432 to 189,780 (from 13 percent to 11 percent of all drug-driven ED visits) between 2004 and 2006.[76]

Marijuana

- Drug legalization advocates in the United States single out marijuana as a different kind of drug, unlike cocaine, heroin, and methamphetamine, because they say it's less dangerous. However, marijuana is not as harmless as some would have you believe.

- Harvard University researchers report that the risk of heart attack is five times higher than usual in the hour after smoking marijuana.[77]

- The National Institute of Health found that a person who smokes five joints per <u>week</u> may be taking in as much tar and cancer-causing chemicals into their lungs as someone who smokes a pack of cigarettes every day.[78]

- Marijuana is much more potent today than in the past. The University of Mississippi found that the average THC (the active ingredient in marijuana} content rose from 2.8 percent (1985) to 10.1 percent (March 2009).[79]

- Smoking marijuana weakens the immune system, [80] and raises the risk of lung infections. [81]

- Other studies indicate that smoked marijuana causes cancer, respiratory problems, increased heart rate, loss of motor skills, and damage to the immune system.

- Yale School of Medicine reports that long- term exposure to marijuana smoking is linked to the same health problems as tobacco smoke, such as daily cough and phlegm production, more frequent acute chest illnesses, a heightened risk of lung infections, and a greater tendency toward obstructed airways. [82]

- The National Multiple Sclerosis Society stated there is no convincing evidence that marijuana benefits people with MS, and does not recommend it as a treatment. [83]

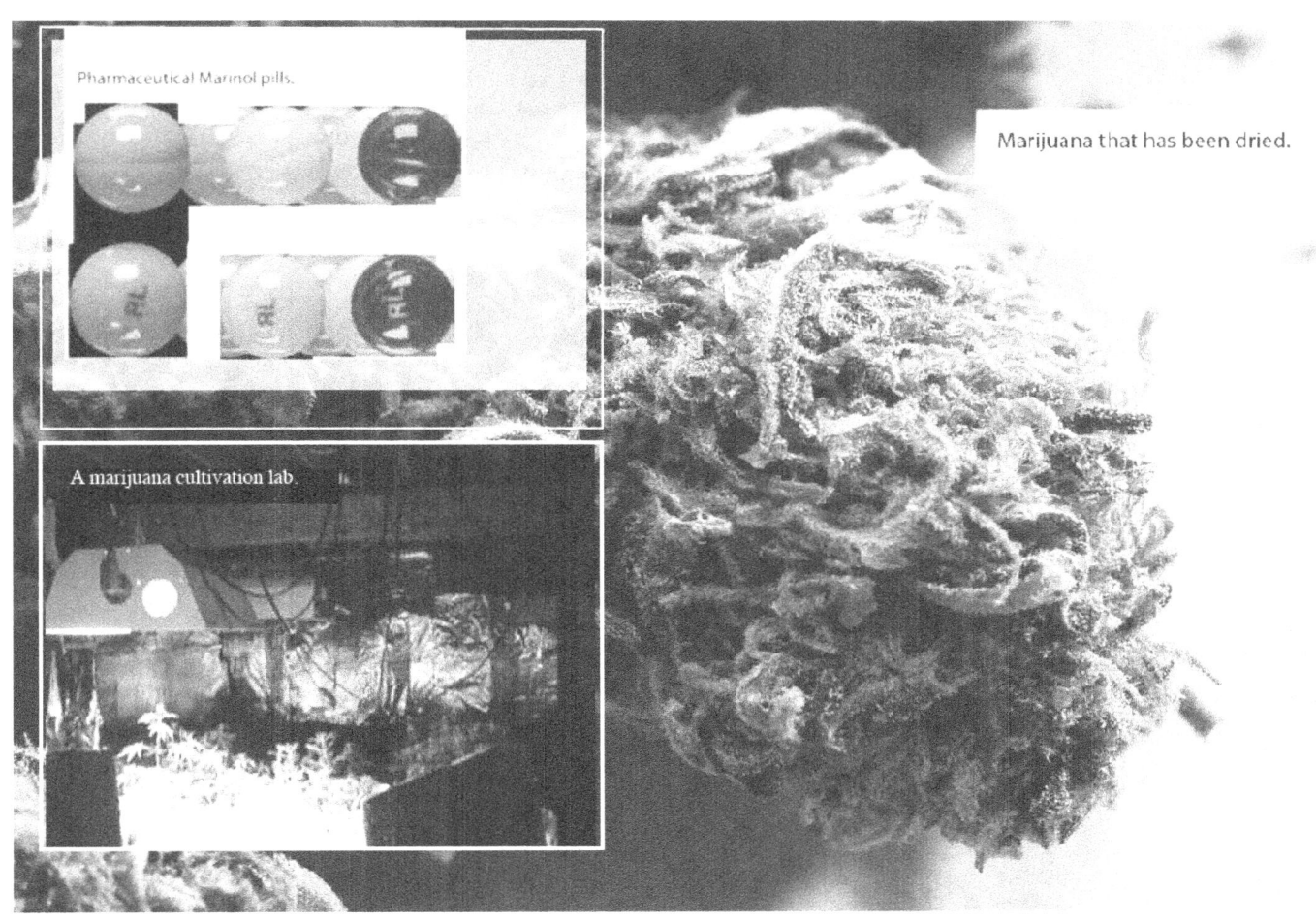

Pharmaceutical Marinol pills.

Marijuana that has been dried.

A marijuana cultivation lab.

- When marijuana is smoked, its effects begin immediately after the drug enters the brain and last from 1 to 3 hours. If marijuana is consumed in food or drink, the short-term effects begin more slowly, usually in 1/2 to 1 hour, and last longer, for as long as 4 hours. Smoking marijuana deposits several times more THC into the blood than does eating or drinking the drug.[84]

- Within a few minutes after inhaling marijuana smoke, an individual's heart begins beating more rapidly, the bronchial passages relax and become enlarged, and blood vessels in the eyes expand, making the eyes look red. The heart rate, normally 70 to 80 beats per minute, may increase by 20 to 50 beats per minute or in some cases even doubles.[85]

- As THC enters the brain, it causes a user to feel euphoric—or "high"—by acting in the brain's reward system, and in areas of the brain that respond to stimuli such as food and drink as well as most drugs of abuse. THC activates the reward system in the same way that nearly all drugs of abuse do, by stimulating brain cells to release the chemical dopamine.[86]

- A marijuana user may experience pleasant sensations, colors and sounds may seem more intense, and time appears to pass very slowly. The user's mouth feels dry, and he or she may suddenly become very hungry and thirsty. His or her hands may tremble and grow cold. The euphoria passes after awhile, and then the user may feel sleepy or depressed. Occasionally, marijuana use produces anxiety, fear, distrust, or panic.[87]

- Cancer of the respiratory tract and lungs may be promoted by marijuana smoke. Marijuana has the potential to promote cancer of the lungs and other parts of the respiratory tract because marijuana smoke contains 50 percent to 70 percent more carcinogenic hydrocarbons than tobacco smoke.[88]

- Marijuana's damage to short-term memory seems to occur because THC alters the way in which information is processed by the hippocampus, a brain area responsible for memory formation. In one study, researchers compared marijuana smoking and nonsmoking 12th-grader's scores on standardized tests of verbal and mathematical skills. Although all of the students had scored equally well in 4th grade, those who were heavy marijuana smokers, (i.e., those who used marijuana seven or more times per week), scored significantly lower in 12th grade than nonsmokers. Another study of 129 college students found that among heavy users of marijuana critical skills related to attention, memory, and learning were significantly impaired, even after they had not used the drug for at least 24 hours.[89]

Fact 4. Smoked marijuana has never been, and will never be scientifically approved for medical use.

- According to the Institute of Medicine, there is no future in smoked marijuana as medicine. However, the prescription drug Marinol—a legal and safe version of medical marijuana which isolates the active ingredient of THC—has been studied and approved by the Food and Drug Administration (FDA) as safe medicine when used as prescribed. The difference between Marinol and smoked marijuana is that you have to get a prescription for Marinol from a licensed physician. You can't buy it on a street corner, and you don't smoke it.

- Unlike smoked marijuana—which contains more than 400 different chemicals, including most of the hazardous chemicals found in tobacco smoke— Marinol has been studied and approved by the medical community and the FDA.

- There are no FDA-approved medications that are smoked. Smoking is generally a poor way to deliver medicine. It is difficult to administer safe, regulated dosages of medicines in smoked form. Secondly, the harmful chemicals and carcinogens that are byproducts of smoking create entirely new health problems. There is four times the level of tar in a marijuana cigarette, for example, than in a tobacco cigarette.

- Morphine, for example, has proven to be a medically valuable drug, but the FDA does not endorse the smoking of opium or heroin. Instead, scientists have extracted active ingredients from opium, which are sold as pharmaceutical products like morphine, codeine, hydrocodone, or oxycodone. In a similar vein, the FDA has not approved smoking marijuana for medicinal purposes, but has approved the active ingredient-THC in the form of scientifically regulated Marinol.

- The DEA helped facilitate the research on Marinol. The National Cancer Institute approached the DEA in the early 1980s regarding their study of THC in relieving nausea and vomiting. As a result, the DEA facilitated the registration and provided regulatory support and guidance for the study. In California, researchers are studying potential uses for marijuana and its ingredients for conditions such as multiple sclerosis and pain. Neither the medical community nor the scientific community has found sufficient data to conclude that smoked marijuana is the best approach to dealing with these important medical issues.

- The most comprehensive, scientifically rigorous review of studies of smoked marijuana was conducted by the Institute of Medicine, an organization chartered by the National Academy of Sciences. In a report released in 1999, the Institute did not recommend the use of smoked marijuana, but did conclude that active ingredients in marijuana could be isolated and developed into a variety of pharmaceuticals, such as Marinol.

- DEA supports ongoing research into potential medicinal uses of marijuana's active ingredients. As of April 2009, there are 123 researchers registered with DEA to perform studies with marijuana, marijuana extracts, and non-tetrahydrocannabinol marijuana derivatives that exist in the plant, such as cannabidiol and cannabinol. Studies include evaluation of abuse potential, physical/psychological effects, adverse effects, therapeutic potential, and detection. Nineteen of the researchers are approved to conduct research with smoked marijuana on human subjects.

Impacts of use on mental health

- A study published in the March 2008 Journal of the American Academy of Child and Adolescent Psychiatry cited the harm of smoking marijuana during pregnancy. The study found a significant relationship between marijuana exposure and child intelligence. Researchers concluded that "prenatal marijuana exposure has a significant effect on school-age intellectual development."[102]

- Doctors at Yale University documented marijuana's damaging effect on the brain after nearly half of 150 healthy volunteers experienced psychotic symptoms, including hallucinations and paranoid delusions, when given THC, the drug's primary active ingredient. The findings were released during a May 2007 international health conference in London.[103]

> *Memory, speed of thinking, and other cognitive abilities get worse over time with marijuana use...*

- American scientists have discovered that the active ingredient in marijuana interferes with synchronized activity between neurons in the hippocampus of rats. The authors of this November 2006 study suggest that action of tetrahydrocannabinol, or THC, might explain why marijuana impairs memory.[104]

- A pair of articles in the *Canadian Journal of Psychiatry* reflect that cannabis use can trigger schizophrenia in people already vulnerable to the mental illness, and assert that this fact should shape marijuana policy.[105]

- Memory, speed of thinking, and other cognitive abilities get worse over time with marijuana use, according to a study published in the March 14, 2006 issue of *Neurology*, the scientific journal of the American Academy of Neurology. The study found that frequent marijuana users performed worse than non-users on tests of cognitive abilities, including divided attention and verbal fluency. Those who had used marijuana for 10 years or more had more problems with their thinking abilities than those who had used marijuana for five-to-10 years. All of the marijuana users were heavy users, which was defined as smoking four or more joints per week.[106]

- According to several recent studies, marijuana use has been linked with depression and suicidal thoughts, in addition to schizophrenia. These studies report that weekly marijuana use among teens doubles the risk of developing depression and triples the incidence of suicidal thoughts.[107]

- Dr. Andrew Campbell, a member of the New South Wales (Australia) Mental Health Review Tribunal, published a study in 2005 which revealed that four out of five individuals with schizophrenia were regular cannabis users when they were teenagers. Between 75-80 percent of the patients involved in the study used cannabis habitually between the ages of 12 and 21.[108] In addition, a laboratory-controlled study by Yale scientists, published in 2004, found that THC "transiently induced a range of schizophrenia-like effects in healthy people."[109]

- Carleton University researchers published a study in 2005 showing that current marijuana users who smoke at least five "joints" per week did significantly worse than non-users when tested on neurocognition tests such as processing speed, memory, and overall IQ.[110]

- Robin Murray, a professor of psychiatry at London's Institute of Psychiatry and consultant at the Maudsley Hospital in London, wrote an editorial which appeared in The Independent, on March 18, 2007, in which he states that the British Government's "mistake was rather to give the impression that cannabis was harmless and that there was no link to psychosis." Based on the fact that "…in the late 1980s and 1990s psychiatrists like me began to see growing numbers of young people with schizophrenia who were taking large amounts of cannabis" Murray claims that "…at least 10 percent of all people with schizophrenia in the UK would not have developed the illness if they had not smoked cannabis." By his estimates, 25,000 individuals have ruined their lives because they smoked cannabis. He also points out that the "skunk" variety of cannabis, which is very popular among young people in Great Britain, contains "15 to 20 percent THC, and new resin preparations have up to 30 percent."[111]

- Dr. John MacLeod, a prominent British psychiatrist states: "If you assume such a link (to schizophrenia with cannabis) then the number of cases of schizophrenia will increase significantly in line with increased use of the drug." He predicts that cannabis use may account for a quarter of all new cases of schizophrenia in three years' time.[112]

- A study from the National Institute of Drug Abuse found that people who smoked marijuana had changes in the blood flow in their brains even after a month of not smoking. The marijuana users had PI (pulsatility index) values somewhat higher than people with chronic high blood pressure and diabetes, which suggests that marijuana use leads to abnormalities in the small blood vessels in the brain. These findings could explain in part the problems with thinking and remembering found in other studies of marijuana users.[113]

- In a presentation on "Neuroimaging Marijuana Use and Effects on Cognitive Function" Professor Krista Lisdahl Medina suggests that chronic heavy marijuana use during adolescence is associated with poorer performance on thinking tasks, including slower psychomotor speed and poorer complex attention, verbal memory, and planning ability. "While recent findings suggest partial recovery of verbal memory functioning within the first three weeks of adolescent abstinence from marijuana, complex attention skills continue to be affected. Not only are their thinking abilities worse, their brain activation to cognitive task is abnormal."[114]

Impacts of marijuana use on physical health

- A long-term study of over 900 New Zealanders by the University of Otago, New Zealand School of Dentistry has found that "heavy marijuana use has been found to contribute to gum disease, apart from the known effects that tobacco smoke was already known to have."[115]

- A study from Monash University and the Alfred Hospital in Australia has found that, "bullous lung disease occurs in marijuana smokers 20 years earlier than tobacco smokers. Often caused by exposure to toxic chemicals or long-term exposure to tobacco smoke, bullae is a condition where air trapped in the lungs causes obstruction to breathing and eventual destruction of the lungs." Dr. Matthew Naughton explains that, "marijuana is inhaled as extremely hot fumes to the peak inspiration and held for as long as possible before slow exhalation. This predisposes the lungs to greater damage, and makes marijuana smokers more prone to bullous disease as compared to cigarette smokers."[116]

> *Bullous lung disease occurs in marijuana smokers 20 years earlier than tobacco smokers.*

- In December 2007 researchers in Canada reported that "marijuana smoke contains significantly higher levels of toxic compounds—including ammonia and hydrogen cyanide—than tobacco smoke and may therefore pose similar health risks. Ammonia levels were 20 times higher in the marijuana smoke than in the tobacco smoke, while hydrogen cyanide, nitric oxide and certain aromatic amines occurred at levels 3-5 times higher in the marijuana smoke."[117]

- Marijuana worsens breathing problems in current smokers with chronic obstructive pulmonary disease (COPD), according to a study released by the American Thoracic Society in May 2007. Among people age 40 and older, smoking cigarettes and marijuana together boosted the odds of developing COPD to 3.5 times the risk of someone who smoked neither.

- According to a 2005 study of marijuana's long-term pulmonary effects by Dr. Donald Tashkin at the University of California, Los Angeles, marijuana smoking deposits significantly more tar and known carcinogens within the tar, such a polycyclic aromatic hydrocarbons, into the airways. In addition to precancerous changes, marijuana smoking is associated with impaired function of the immune system components in the lungs.[127]

- Scientists at Sweden's Karolinska Institute, a medical university, have advanced their understanding of how smoking marijuana during pregnancy may damage the fetal brain. Findings from their study, released in May 2007, explain how endogenous cannabinoids exert adverse effects on nerve cells, potentially imposing life-long cognitive and motor deficits in afflicted new born babies.[119]

- According to new research from Vanderbilt University the use of marijuana by women trying to conceive or those recently becoming pregnant is not recommended, as it endangers the passage of the embryo from the ovary to the uterus and can result in a failed pregnancy. A study with mice has shown that marijuana exposure may compromise the pregnancy outcome because an active ingredient in marijuana, tetrahydrocannabinol (THC), interferes with a fertilized egg's ability to implant in the lining of the uterus.[125]

- Infants exposed to marijuana in the womb show subtle behavioral changes in their first days of life, according to researchers in Brazil. The newborns were more irritable than non-exposed infants, less responsive, and more difficult to calm. They also cried more, startled more easily, and were jitterier. Such changes have the potential to interfere with the mother-child bonding process. "It is necessary to counter the misconception that marijuana is a 'benign drug' and to educate women regarding the risks and possible consequences related to its use during pregnancy," Dr. Marina Carvahlo de Moraes Barros and her colleagues concluded.[126]

- A 2007 study from New Zealand reports that cannabis smoking may cause five percent of lung cancer cases in that country.[120]

- Researchers at the Fred Hutchinson Cancer Research Center in Seattle found that frequent or long-term marijuana use may significantly increase a man's risk of developing the most aggressive type of testicular cancer, nonseminoma. Nonseminoma is a fast-growing testicular malignancy that tends to strike early, between the ages of 20 and 35, and accounts for about 40 percent of all testicular-cancer cases."[121]

- While smoking tobacco cigarettes is known to be a major risk factor for the bladder cancer most common among people age 60 and older, researchers are now finding a correlation between smoking marijuana and bladder cancer. In a study of younger patients with transitional cell bladder cancer, Dr. Martha Terriss found that 88.5 percent had a history of smoking marijuana.

- Marijuana smoke has many of the same carcinogen-containing tars as cigarettes and may get even more of them into the body because marijuana cigarettes are unfiltered and users tend to hold the smoke in their lungs for prolonged periods. Dr. Terriss notes that more research is needed, but does recommend that doctors who find blood in a young patient's urine sample follow-up with questions about marijuana use, and more strongly consider ruling out bladder cancer as the cause.[122]

- According to a review of decades of research on marijuana smoking and lung cancer, smoking marijuana can cause changes in lung tissue that may promote cancer growth. However, it is not possible to directly link pot use to lung cancer based on existing evidence. Nevertheless, researchers indicate that the precancerous changes seen in studies included in their analysis, as well as the fact that marijuana smokers generally inhale more deeply and hold smoke in their lungs longer than cigarette smokers, and that marijuana is smoked without a filter, do suggest that smoking marijuana could indeed boost lung cancer risk. It is known, they add, that marijuana smoking deposits more tar in the lungs than cigarette smoking does.[123]

• Smoking three cannabis joints will cause you to inhale the same amount of toxic chemicals as a whole pack of cigarettes, according to researchers from the French National Consumers' Institute. Cannabis smoke contains seven times more tar and carbon monoxide than cigarette smoke. Someone smoking a joint of cannabis resin rolled with tobacco will inhale twice the amount of benzene and three times as much toluene as if they were smoking a regular cigarette.[124]

• Smoked marijuana is associated with an increased risk of the same respiratory symptoms as tobacco, including coughing, phlegm production, chronic bronchitis, shortness of breath and wheezing. Because cannabis plants are contaminated with a range of fungal spores, smoking marijuana may also increase the risk of respiratory exposure by infectious organisms (i.e., molds and fungi).[128]

• In its October, 2006, issue of *NIDA Notes*, Dr. Tashkin notes that. "Biopsies of bronchial tissue provide evidence that regular marijuana smoking injures airway epithelial cells, leading to dysregulation of bronchial epithelial cell growth and eventually to possible malignant changes... moreover, marijuana smoking deposits significantly more tar and known carcinogens within the tar, such as polycyclic aromatic hydrocarbons, in the airways than tobacco." In addition to precancerous changes, Dr. Tashkin found that" marijuana smoking is associated with a range of damaging pulmonary effects, including inhibition of the tumor-killing and bactericidal activity of alveolar macrophages, the primary immune cells within the lung."[130]

• Legalization advocates claim that the United States has wasted billions of dollars in its anti-drug efforts. But for those saved from drug addiction, these are hardly wasted dollars. Compared to the social costs of drug abuse and addiction—whether in taxpayer dollars, or in pain and suffering—government spending on drug control is minimal.

- The **American Medical Association (AMA)** has always endorsed "well-controlled" studies of marijuana and related cannabinoids in patients with serious conditions for which preclinical, anecdotal, or controlled evidence suggests efficacy and the application of such results to the understanding and treatment of disease." In November 2009, the AMA amended its policy, urging that maruijuana's status as a Schedule I controlled substance be reviewed "with the goal of facilitating the conduct of clinical research and development of cannabinoid-based medicines, and alternate delivery methods." The AMA also stated that "this should not be viewed as an endorsement of state-based medical cannibis programs, the leagalization of marijuana, or the scientific evidence on the therapeutic use of cannibis meets the current standards for prescription drug product.[90]

- The **American Cancer Society** "does not advocate inhaling smoke, nor the legalization of marijuana," although the organization does support carefully controlled clinical studies for alternative delivery methods, specifically a THC skin patch.[91]

- The **American Academy of Pediatrics** believes that "any change in the legal status of marijuana, even if limited to adults, could affect the prevalence of use among adolescents." While it supports scientific research on the possible medical use of cannabinoids as opposed to smoked marijuana, it opposes the legalization of marijuana.[92]

- The **National Multiple Sclerosis Society** has stated that it could not recommend that medical marijuana be made widely available for people with multiple sclerosis for symptom management, explaining: "This decision was not only based on existing legal barriers to its use but, even more importantly, because studies to date do not demonstrate a clear benefit compared to existing symptomatic therapies and because issues of side effects, systemic effects, and long-term effects are not yet clear."[93]

- In a reversal of their 2006 official position, the **Australian Medical Association (AMA)** has called on the state government of Western Australia to introduce harsher marijuana laws. The AMA cited a recent review of international research on the links between marijuana and mental illness. AMA president Dr. Rosanna Capolingua said that "soft marijuana laws certainly do not help support the message that marijuana is not a soft drug."[94]

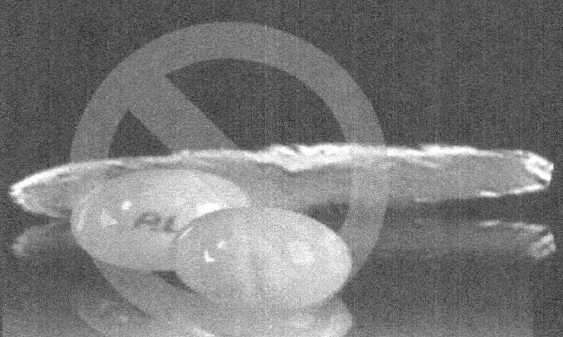

- **The United Nations Economic and Social Council** has expressed concern about the trend towards the development of lenient policies relating to cannabis and other drugs that are not in accordance with international drug control treaties; and that such trends may have a negative impact on efforts being made to eradicate cannabis cultivation and combat drug trafficking.[95]

- **The International Narcotics Control Board** issued a statement urging other countries to consider the real dangers of cannabis. "…cannabis is classified under international conventions as a drug with a number of personal and public health problems. It is not a 'soft' drug as some people would have you believe. There is new evidence confirming well-known mental health problems, and some countries with a more liberal policy towards cannabis are reviewing their position. Countries need to take a strong stance towards cannabis abuse."[96]

- **The British Medical Association (BMA)** voiced extreme concern that downgrading the criminal status of marijuana would "mislead" the public into believing that the drug is safe. The BMA maintains that marijuana "has been linked to greater risk of heart disease, lung cancer, bronchitis and emphysema."[97] The 2004 Deputy Chairman of the BMA's Board of Science said that "[t]he public must be made aware of the harmful effects we know result from smoking this drug."[98] Unfortunately, the British Government did not heed their Medical Association's warning and downgraded cannabis from Class B to a Class C drug in 2004. This resulted in an increase of crime and various health problems, which later prompted a reversal, according to United Kingdom's Home Office.[99] As a result, on May 8, 2008, the Home Office announced that cannabis will be reclassified as a Class B drug.[100]

Fact 5: Drug control spending is a minor portion of the U.S. budget. Compared to the social costs of drug abuse and addiction, government spending on drug control is minimal.

Social Costs

- In 2002, drug abuse cost American society an estimated $181 billion.[132] More important were the losses that are imperfectly symbolized by those billions of dollars—the destruction of lives, the damage of addiction, fatalities from car accidents, illness, and lost opportunities and dreams.

Loss of life

- The number of drug overdose deaths in the United States continues to increase, representing a serious threat to public health. To a significant extent, these deaths are related to increases in prescription drug abuse. Rates of overdose deaths are currently four to five times higher than during the black tar heroin epidemic of the mid-1970s, and more than twice the rates during the peak years of crack cocaine in the early 1990s. In 2005 there were 22,400 drug overdose deaths in the United States, compared to approximately 17,000 homicides in the same year.[133]

- According to a report in the February 9, 2007 Morbidity and Mortality Weekly Report, "In 2004, poisoning was second only to motor-vehicle crashes as a cause of death from unintentional injury in the United States. Nearly all poisoning deaths in the United States are attributed to drugs, and most drug poisonings result from the abuse of prescription and illegal drugs."

- The CDC determined that poisoning mortality rates in the United States increased 62.5 percent a year from 1999 to 2004. The increase in deaths because of unintentional poisoning occurred almost exclusively among those whose deaths were attributed to unintentional drug poisoning. By 2004, drug poisoning accounted for 19,838 deaths, or 94.7 percent of all unintentional poisoning deaths.[134]

- In 2006, an estimated 8.3 percent of Americans aged 12 or older were current (past month) illicit drug users, resulting in over 38,000 deaths from drug-induced causes. By comparison, there were just over 125 million (or 50.9 percent of all Americans) current alcohol users and just over 22,000 deaths due to alcohol-induced causes.[135]

- Legalization would result in skyrocketing costs that would be paid by American taxpayers and consumers. Legalization would significantly increase drug use and addiction—and all the social costs that go with it. With the removal of the social and legal sanctions against drugs, many experts estimate the user population would at least double. For example, a 1994 article in the New England Journal of Medicine stated that it was probable, that if cocaine were legalized, the number of cocaine addicts in America would increase from two million to at least 20 million.

- If we were to regulate marijuana or other drugs, we would have to agree that it's acceptable for society to profit from a person's addiction. There were approximately 38,000 overdose deaths for illicit drugs and non-medical use of prescription drugs in 2006 according to the Center for Disease Control.[136] How much are those lives worth?

Related Health Care Costs

- Drug abuse drives some of America's most costly social problems—including domestic violence, child abuse, chronic mental illness, the spread of AIDS, and homelessness. Drug treatment costs, hospitalization for long-term drug-related disease, and treatment of the consequences of family violence burden our already strapped health care system.

- In 2006, there were more than 1,742,887 hospital emergency department drug misuse or abuse admissions in the United States.[137]

- "Substance abuse is the most commonly reported modifiable behavior impeding TB elimination efforts in the United States," according to an analysis of tuberculosis cases reported to the Center for Disease Control and Prevention between 1997 and 2006. Nearly one-fifth of the patients reported substance abuse in the year before their TB was diagnosed.[138]

- The Centers for Disease Control and Prevention has estimated that 36 percent of new HIV cases are directly or indirectly linked to injecting drug users.[139] Drug abuse and addiction have been linked with HIV/AIDS since the beginning of the epidemic. While intravenous drug use is well known in this regard, less recognized is the role that drug abuse plays more generally in the spread of HIV – the virus that causes AIDS – by increasing the likelihood of high-risk sex with infected partners. This is because the addictive and intoxicating effects of many drugs, which can alter judgment and inhibition, and lead people to engage in impulsive and unsafe behaviors.[140]

Treatment Needs

- In 2008, an estimated 22.2 million persons aged 12 or older were classified with substance dependence or abuse (8.9 percent of the population aged 12 or older). Of these, 3.1 million were classified with dependence on or abuse of both alcohol and illicit drugs; 3.9 million were dependent on or abused illicit drugs but not alcohol; and 15.2 million were dependent on or abused alcohol but not illicit drugs.141

- There were 23.1 million persons aged 12 or older in need of treatment for illicit drug or alcohol use. Of these, only 2.3 million people received treatment at a specialty facility. That means that 20.8 million people who needed treatment from a specialty facility did not receive it.[142] If we do not have the resources to treat all the people who are substance abusers how will we handle the increased workload generated with the legalization of illicit drugs?

Workplace

- The American workplace bears many significant costs resulting from alcohol and drug abuse. The 2007 there were 20.4 million adults classified with substance abuse or dependence, 60.4 percent (12.3 million) of them were employed full time. Of the estimated 17.4 million adult users of illicit drugs 18 or older, 75 percent (13.1 million people) are employed either full or part-time. These figures underscore the costs of substance use in the workforce, including accidents and injuries, absenteeism, low morale, and productivity losses.[143]

- In addition, legalization—and the increased addiction it would spawn—would result in lost workforce productivity and the unpredictable damage that it would cause to the American economy. In 2002, productivity losses due to drug abuse cost the economy almost $128.6 billion.[144]

- Drug use by workers leads not only to more unexcused absences and higher job turnover rates, but also presents an enormous safety problem in the workplace.[145] Nearly twice as many current illicit drug users skipped one or more days of work due to illness or injury in the past month compared to workers who did not abuse drugs.[146]

- There has been some success with reducing the use of drugs in the workplace. Effective drug free workplace programs are helping to reduce substance abuse among the workforce by letting workers know that drug use is not acceptable and by offering help to those that need it. Drug testing programs have contributed to the decline in illicit drug use, including cocaine and methamphetamine. Over the past twenty years, positive drug test results declined from 13.6 percent in 1988 to 3.6 percent in 2008.[147]

Traffic Accidents

- In 2007, over 1.4 million drivers were arrested for driving under the influence of alcohol <u>and</u> narcotics. Drugs other than alcohol are involved in about 18 percent of motor vehicle driver deaths. These other drugs are generally used in combination with alcohol.[148]

o   According to a study published in *Traffic Injury Prevention*, more than half of motor vehicle crash drivers tested positive for drugs other than alcohol in a Level-1 trauma center. In a 90-day study, nearly two-thirds of trauma center admissions were victims of motor vehicle crashes (MVC). Blood and urine was collected from 168 MVC victims of whom 108 were identified as the driver in the crash. Toxicology results indicated that 65.7 percent of drivers tested positive for either commonly abused drugs or alcohol. More than half of the drivers tested positive for drugs (51percent) other than alcohol, with one in four drivers testing positive for marijuana use. [149] Studies drawing similar conclusions about the connection between drug use and traffic accidents were in studies conducted in Australia,[150] British Columbia,[151] and France.[152]

o   An issue of the *Morbidity and Mortality Weekly Report*, published in December of 2006, reported that of the 784 motor vehicle fatalities that took place in West Virginia 2004-2005. Almost half (47.3 percent) of all those victums tested positive for alcohol or drugs, 11.1 percent tested positive for both, and more than one quarter (26 percent) of those who died tested positive for drug use.[153]

• Every day, 36 people in the U.S. die, and approximately 700 more are injured, in motor vehicle crashes that involve an alcohol-impaired driver. The annual cost of alcohol-related crashes totals more than $51 billion.[154] According to the National Highway Traffic Safety Administration, vehicle accidents are the leading cause of death among young people age 16-20.[155] If we legalized drugs and had more impaired drivers on the road, what would the increased cost in lives and dollars be?

• In 2008 there were 10 million persons aged 12 and older who reported driving under the influence of illicit drugs during the past year. The rate was highest among young adults aged 18 to 25.[156]

• According to the National Institute on Drug Abuse funded study, a large number of American adolescents are putting themselves and others at great risk by driving under the influence of illicit drugs or alcohol. In 2006, 30 percent of high school seniors reported driving after drinking heavily or using drugs, or riding in a car whose driver had been drinking heavily or using drugs, at least once in the prior two weeks.

• Dr. Patrick O'Malley, lead author of the study, observed that "driving under the influence is not an alcohol-only problem. In 2006, 13 percent of seniors said they drove after using marijuana while ten percent drove after having five or more drinks."

- "Vehicle accidents are the leading cause of death among those aged 15 to 20," added Dr. Nora Volkow, Director of NIDA. "Combining the lack of driving experience among teens with the use of marijuana and/or other substances that impair cognitive and motor abilities can be a deadly combination."[157] Can we afford to legalize drugs and increase the percent of youth driving under the influence?

Family Problems

- More than 8.3 million children under 18 years of age lived with at least one parent who was dependent on or abused alcohol, and/or an illicit drug this past year. Of these, almost 7.3 million lived with a parent who was dependent on or abused alcohol and about 2.1 million lived with a parent who is dependent on or abused illicit drugs. This means that more than 1 in 10 children in the United States under the age of 18 live with a substance-dependent or substance-abusing parent.[158]

- "The research increasingly shows that children growing up in a home with alcohol-and drug-abusing parents suffer – often greatly," according to SAMHSA Acting Administrator Eric Broderick. "The chronic emotional stress in such an environment can damage their social and emotional development and permanently impede healthy brain development, often resulting in mental and physical health problems across the lifespan. This underlines the importance of preventive interventions at the earliest possible age."[159]

- According to the 2005 National Center on Addiction and Substance Abuse Report, alcohol and drug abuse are diseases with severe consequences for all family members, particularly children. Children of substance abusing parents are likelier to become substance abusers themselves. Alcohol and drug-abusing parents are three times likelier to abuse their children and four times likelier to neglect them than parents who do not abuse these substances. Children of alcohol and drug abusers are at increased risk of accidents, injuries, and academic failure. Such children are more likely to suffer conduct disorders, depression or anxiety, conditions that also increase the risk that children will drink and use drugs themselves.[160]

- Substance abusers' households tend to be high in conflict, likelier than others to include yelling, insults, and serious arguments. Substance abusing parents tend to engage in fewer family activities with their children. Parental substance abuse is one of the main problems facing families who are reported for child endangerment. Parental substance abuse increases the incidence of family violence, divorce, financial problems, and exposure to crime. [161]

- There is even greater risk to children whose parents use and manufacture methamphetamine. Methamphetamine abusers often produce the drug in their own homes and apartments, using hazardous chemicals such as hydrochloric acid, iodine, and anhydrous ammonia. Children who inhabit such homes often inhale dangerous fumes and gases and ingest toxic chemicals or illicit drugs. These children commonly test positive for methamphetamine, and suffer from short and long-term health consequences. They are also often neglected, leading to psychological and developmental problems. In 2004 U.S. law enforcement agencies report having seized 9,895, illicit methamphetamine laboratories in 2004. These agencies report that 2,474 children were affected by these laboratories (i.e., they were exposed to chemicals, they resided at laboratory sites, or they were displaced from their homes).[162]

• A study by Rand Corporation estimates that methamphetamine cost American society $23.4 billion in 2005.

Tax, Sale, and Advertising Consequences

• Advocates argue that legalization will lower prices for drugs. But that raises a dilemma: If the price of drugs is low, many more people will be able to afford them and the demand for drugs will explode. For example, if the cost of cocaine production is as low as $3 per gram and is sold at retail price, a single unit could be bought for as little as ten cents. That means a young person could buy six hits of cocaine for the price of a candy bar. On the other hand, if legal drugs are priced too high, through excise taxes, for example, illegal traffickers will be able to undercut them.

• Advocates of legalization argue that a legal market could be limited to those above a certain age level, as it is for alcohol and cigarettes. Those under the age limits would therefore not be permitted to buy drugs at authorized outlets. But teenagers today have found many ways to circumvent age restrictions, whether by using false identification, or by buying liquor and cigarettes from older friends. According to the 2007 SAMSHA National Household Survey on Drug Abuse, there were 4.6 million persons aged 12 or older who had used alcohol for the first time within the past 12 months; this averages to approximately 12,500 initiates per day. Most of the 4.6 million (85.9 percent) recent initiates were younger than 21 at the time of initiation.[164] With drugs, teenagers would have an additional outlet: the highly organized illegal trafficking networks that would undoubtedly concentrate their marketing efforts on young people to make up for the business they lost to legal outlets.

• Alcohol and tobacco have proven harmful, addictive, and difficult to regulate. Alcohol is the third leading cause of death in the United States—each year over 100,000 Americans die of alcohol-related causes. The Surgeon General estimates that problems resulting from alcohol use and abuse cost society almost $200 billion every year, and these costs are far higher than revenue generated by alcohol taxes.[165]

• Tobacco, the other substance that often is suggested as a model for how we could have 'legal' marijuana, offers a picture of a similarly bleak future. The Center for Disease Control estimates that the total economic costs associated with cigarette smoking is approximately $7.18 per pack of cigarettes. The tax revenue generated to cover these costs? The federal excise tax is $1.01 per pack of cigarettes.[166] The median state cigarette excise tax rate, as of January 1, 2007, is 80 cents.[167] This hardly sounds like the "economic windfall" that will cure our budget woes.

Costs to the Taxpayer

- In FY 2009, the total federal drug control budget requested was $14.8 billion.[168] In comparison, the Department of Education's FY 2009 budget request was almost 10 times this amount: $137.6 billion.[169] Education is a long-term social concern, with new problems that arise with every new generation. The same can be said of drug abuse and addiction. Yet nobody suggests that we should give up on our children's education. Why, then, would we give up on helping to keep them off drugs and free from addiction?

- On the surface, advocates of legalization present an appealing, but simplistic, argument that by legalizing drugs we can move vast sums of money from enforcing drug laws to solving society's ills. But as in education and drug addiction, vast societal problems can't be solved overnight. It takes time, focus, persistence – and resources.

- Legalization advocates fail to note the skyrocketing social and welfare costs, not to mention the misery and addiction that would accompany the outright legalization of drugs.

- Legalization advocates also fail to mention that, unless drugs are made available to children, law enforcement will still be needed to deal with the sale of drugs to minors. In other words, a vast black market will still exist. Since young people are often the primary target of pushers, many of the criminal organizations that now profit from illegal drugs would continue to do so.

- Furthermore, it is reasonable to assume that the health and societal costs of drug legalization would also increase exponentially. Drug treatment costs, hospitalization for long-term drug-related diseases, and treatment of family violence would also place additional demands on our already overburdened health care system. More taxes would have to be raised to pay for a system already bursting at the seams.

- Criminal justice costs would likely increase if drugs were legalized. It is quite likely that violent crime would significantly increase with greater accessibility to dangerous drugs—whether the drugs themselves are legal or not. In 2004, one in four violent offenders in prison committed their offenses under the influence of drugs.[170] More taxes would have to be raised to pay for additional law enforcement personnel, which is already overburdened by crimes and traffic fatalities associated with alcohol. Law enforcement is already challenged by significant alcohol-related crimes. More users would probably result in the commission of additional crimes, causing incarceration costs to increase as well.

- A 2004 study by the Bureau of Justice Statistics of federal and state prisoners measured drug dependence and abuse for the first time. Fifty-three percent of state and 45 percent of federal prisoners met the criteria for drug dependence or abuse.[171]

Fact 6: Legalization of drugs will lead to increased use and increased levels of addiction.

- Legalization proponents claim that making illegal drugs legal would not cause more of these substances to be consumed, nor would addiction increase. They claim that many people can use drugs in moderation, and that many would choose not to use drugs, just as many abstain from alcohol and tobacco now. Yet how much misery is already attributable to alcoholism and smoking?

- It's clear from history that periods of lax controls are accompanied by more drug abuse, and that periods of tight controls are accompanied by less drug abuse.

  o During the 19th century, morphine was legally refined from opium and hailed as a miracle drug. However, many soldiers on both sides of the Civil War who were given morphine for their wounds became addicted to it. In 1880, many drugs, including opium and cocaine, were legal — and like some drugs today were seen as benign medicine not requiring a doctor's care and oversight and addiction skyrocketed.

  o By 1900, about one American in 200 was either a cocaine or opium addict. Among the reforms of this era was the federal Pure Food and Drug Act of 1906, which required manufacturers of patent medicines to reveal the contents of the drugs they sold. In this way, Americans learned which of their medicines contained heavy doses of cocaine and opiates — drugs they had now learned to avoid.

  o Specific federal drug legislation and oversight began with the 1914 Harrison Act, the first broad anti-drug law in the United States. Enforcement of this law contributed to a significant decline in narcotic addiction in the United States. Addiction in the United States eventually fell to its lowest level during World War II, when the number of addicts was estimated at somewhere between 20,000 and 40,000. Many addicts, faced with disappearing supplies, were forced to give up their drug habits.

Failed Legalization Ventures

- In 1975, the Alaska Supreme Court ruled that the state could not interfere with an adult's possession of marijuana for personal consumption in the home. The court's ruling became a green light for marijuana use. Although the ruling was limited to persons 19 and over, teens were among those increasingly using marijuana. According to a 1988 University of Alaska study, the state's 12 to 17-year-olds used marijuana at more than twice the national average for their age group. Alaska's residents voted in 1990 to re-criminalize possession of marijuana.175

- By 1979, after 11 states decriminalized marijuana and the Carter administration had considered federal decriminalization, marijuana use shot up among teenagers. That year, almost 51 percent of 12th graders reported they used marijuana in the last 12 months. By 1992, with tougher laws and increased attention to the risks of drug abuse, that figure had been reduced to 22 percent, a 57-percent decline.[176]

- Other countries have also had this experience. The Netherlands has had its own troubles with increased use of cannabis products. From 1984 to 1996, the Dutch liberalized the use of cannabis. Surveys reveal that lifetime prevalence of cannabis in Holland increased consistently and sharply during those years. For the age group 18-20, the increase went from 15 percent in 1984 to 44 percent in 1996. [177]

- The Netherlands is not alone. Switzerland, with some of the most liberal drug policies in Europe, experimented with what became known as "Needle Park". Needle Park became a mecca for drug addicts throughout Europe. It was an area where addicts could come to openly purchase drugs and inject heroin without police intervention or control. Because of the rapid decline in the neighborhood surrounding Needle Park, with increased crime and violence, led authorities to finally close it in 1992.[178]

Alcohol and tobacco costs

- What is disconcerting is that alcohol and tobacco are often pointed to as 'models' for how the government could regulate the use of marijuana. This suggestion ignores the significant costs that society pays because of the ease of availability of alcohol and tobacco.

- The relationship between legalization and increased use becomes evident when you consider two current "legal drugs," tobacco and alcohol. The number of users of these "legal drugs" is far greater than the number of users of illegal drugs. The 2008 National Household Survey on Drug Abuse reports an estimated 129 million Americans used alcohol at least once a month. About 70.9 million Americans used tobacco at the same rate. But less than 20.1 million Americans used illegal drugs at least once a month.[179]

Alcohol costs to society

- According to the National Institute on Alcohol Abuse and Alcoholism, millions of Americans are heavy drinkers and they have a greater risk of liver disease, heart disease, sleep disorders, depression, stroke, bleeding from the stomach, sexually transmitted infections from unsafe sex, and several types of cancer. Heavy drinkers may also have problems managing diabetes, high blood pressure, and other conditions.[180]

- The Centers for Disease Control estimates that between 2001 and 2005, there were approximately 79,000 deaths annually due to excessive alcohol use,[181] making excessive alcohol use the third leading cause of death in the United States.[182]

- The economic cost of alcohol abuse was about $185 billion in 1998, which translated into roughly $683 for every man, woman, and child living in the United States.[183]

Tobacco costs to society

- Tobacco, the other substance that is often suggested as a model for how we could have 'legal' marijuana, offers a picture of a similarly bleak future. According to the Surgeon General, tobacco is the leading preventable cause of death in the United States.[184] Cigarette smoking causes an estimated 438,000 deaths, or about one of every five deaths, each year—including approximately 38,000 deaths from secondhand smoke exposure.[185,186]

- During 2000-2004, cigarette smoking was estimated to be responsible for $193 billion in annual health-related economic losses in the United States ($96 billion in direct medical costs and approximately and $97 billion in lost productivity).[187] This translates to an estimated total economic cost of $10.47 per pack of cigarettes sold in the United States.[188]

- How much tax revenue is generated to cover the cost of tobacco use? In 2008, the average retail price of a pack of cigarettes in the United States was $4.35 (including federal, state, and municipal taxes).[189] The median state cigarette excise tax rate, as of January 1, 2008, was $1.[190] The federal cigarette tax is $1.01.[191] This hardly sounds like the "economic windfall" that will cure our budget woes.

- If we were to regulate marijuana, we would agree that it's acceptable for society to profit from a person's addiction. There were approximately 38,000 overdose deaths for illicit drugs and non-medical use of prescription drugs for 2006 according to the Center for Disease Control.[192] Legalization would multiply the cost by greatly adding to the class of drug-addicted Americans. To put it in perspective, less than 8 percent of the population uses illegal drugs of any kind. That's 19 million regular users of all illegal drugs, compared to 71 million tobacco users, and over 127 million alcohol users.[193] How much are those lives worth?

- Use of illicit drugs and alcohol is more common among current cigarette smokers than nonsmokers. Among persons aged 12 or older, 20.4 percent of past month cigarette smokers reported current use of an illicit drug compared with 4.2 percent of persons who were not current cigarette smokers in 2008. Past month alcohol use was reported by 67.4 percent of current cigarette smokers compared with 46.7 percent of those who did not use cigarettes in the past month. The association also was found with binge drinking (44.6 percent of current cigarette users vs. 16.5 percent of current nonusers) and heavy drinking (16.8 vs. 3.8 percent, respectively).[194]

- It's clear that there is a relationship between legalization and increasing drug use, and that legalization would result in an unacceptably high number of drug-addicted Americans.

- When legalization advocates suggest that easy access to drugs won't contribute to greater levels of addiction, they aren't being candid. The question isn't whether legalization will increase addiction levels—it will— it's whether we care or not. The compassionate response is to do everything possible to prevent the destruction that addiction causes, not make it easier to harm ourselves, our community and our future.

Fact 7: Crime, violence, and drug use go hand-in-hand.

- Proponents of legalization have many theories regarding the connection between drugs and violence, claiming that drug use is a victimless crime, that users are putting only themselves in harm's way, and as a result have a right to use drugs.

- Other proponents of legalization contend that if drugs were legalized, crime and violence would decrease, believing that it is the illegal nature of drug production, trafficking, and use that fuels crime and violence, rather than the violent and irrational behavior that drugs themselves prompt. Proponents state that users commit crimes to pay for drugs because they are not easily obtained, and if drugs were legal, profits associated with drugs because of their illegal status would disappear, and the black market and criminal activity of traffikers would be eliminated.

  o Yet, under a legalization scenario, a black market for drugs would still exist, and it would be a vast black market. If drugs were legal for those over 18 or 21, there would be a market for everyone under that age. People under the age of 21 consume the majority of illegal drugs, so an illegal market and organized crime to supply it would remain—along with the organized crime that profits from it.

  o If only marijuana were legalized, drug traffickers would continue to traffic in heroin and cocaine. In either case, drug-related violence would not be ended by legalization.

  o If only marijuana, cocaine, and heroin were legalized, there would still be a market for PCP and methamphetamine. Where do legalizers want to draw the line? Or do they support legalizing all drugs, no matter how addictive and dangerous?

- Drug use often causes an individual to do things they normally wouldn't do if they were free of the influence of drugs. The greatest weakness in the logic of legalizers is that the violence associated with drugs is simply a product of drug trafficking. That is, if drugs were legal, then most drug crime would end. But violent crime is often committed not because people want to buy drugs, but because people use drugs. Drug use changes behavior and exacerbates criminal activity.

Drug use and crime

- Scientific studies support the connection between drug use and crime. Drug users are not only harming themselves, they are harming anyone who may have the misfortune of crossing their path. Dr. Mitchell Rosenthal, head of Phoenix House, a major drug treatment center, has pointed out that, "there are a substantial number of abusers who cross the line from permissible self-destruction to becoming 'driven' people who are 'out of control' and put others in danger of their risk-taking, violence, abuse, or HIV infection."[195]

- In the 2004 Survey of Inmates in state and federal correctional facilities, 32 percent of state prisoners and 26 percent of federal prisoners said they had committed their current offense while under the influence of drugs. Among state prisoners, drug offenders (44 percent) and property offenders (39 percent) reported the highest incidence of drug use at the time of the offense. Among federal prisoners, drug offenders (32 percent) and violent offenders (24 percent) were the most likely to report drug use at the time of their crimes.[196]

- Research clearly demonstrates that marijuana has the potential to cause problems in daily life and make a person's existing problems worse. In one study, heavy marijuana abusers reported that the drug impaired several important measures of life achievement including physical and mental health, cognitive abilities, social life, and career status.[197] Several studies associate workers' marijuana smoking with increased absences, tardiness, accidents, workers' compensation claims, and job turnover.[198]

- Results from NIDA's Monitoring the Future survey indicate that in 2006 more than 13 percent of high school seniors admitted to driving under the influence of marijuana in the weeks prior to the survey.[199] Marijuana intoxication can cause distorted perceptions, impaired coordination, difficulty in thinking and problem solving, and problems with learning and memory. Research has shown that marijuana's adverse impact on learning and memory can last for days or weeks after the acute effects of the drug wear off.[200] As a result, someone who smokes marijuana every day may be functioning at a suboptimal intellectual level <u>all</u> of the time.

Victims of Drug Crimes

- Drug-related crime victimization occurs in many forms. Many drug users resort to violent crimes that include homicide, assault, and armed robbery. Drug use may contribute to situations such as domestic violence. In an attempt to obtain their drug of choice, drug users may also commit non-violent crimes, such as identity theft.

- The National Center on Addiction and Substance Abuse at Columbia University estimates in a 2005 report that substance abuse is a factor in at least 70 percent of all reported cases of child maltreatment. Adults with substance abuse disorders are 2.7 times more likely to report abusive behavior and 4.2 times more likely to report neglectful behavior toward their children.[201]

> Adults with substance abuse disorders are 2.7 times more likely to report abusive behavior, and 4.2 times more likely to report neglectful beharvior towards children.

- Maltreated children of substance abusing parents are more likely to have poorer physical, intellectual, social, and emotional outcomes and are at a greater risk of developing substance abuse problems themselves.[202]

- Children often test positive for the drug of their parent's choice. For example, child endangerment was charged in a case where a child was present in a home with ongoing marijuana cultivation and processing. Also, in a separate situation, child abuse was reported after a child tested positive for marijuana as a result of passive inhalation when marijuana smoke was blown into a child's face so they would go to sleep.

- According to the National Crime Victimization Survey (NCVS), there were 5.2 million violent victimizations in the U.S. age 12 or older in 2007. Victims of violence were asked to describe whether they perceived the offender to have been drinking or using drugs. In 27 percent of the cases victims of violence reported that the offender was using drugs or alcohol.[203]

- The Uniform Crime Reporting Program (UCR) of the Federal Bureau of Investigation (FBI) reported that in 2006 5.3 percent of the 14,990 homicides committed that year were narcotics related.[204]

Drug use and violence

- Drug use, crime, and violence go hand in hand. In 2004, 17 percent of state prisoners and 18 percent of federal inmates said they committed their current offense to obtain money for drugs. [205]

- In 2002, about 25 percent of convicted property and drug offenders in local jails had committed their crimes to get money for drugs, compared to 5 percent of violent and public order offenders. Among state prisoners in 2004 the pattern was similar, with property (30 percent) and drug offenders (26 percent) more likely to commit their crimes for drug money than violent (10 percent) and public-order offenders (7 percent). In federal prisons property offenders (11 percent) were less than half as likely as drug offenders (25 percent) to report drug money as a motive in their offenses.[206]

Figure 1 Percent of Prison and Jail Inmates Who Committed Offense to Get Money for Drugs[207]

	Local Jail Inmates	State Prisoners	Federal Prisoners
	2002	2004	2004
Total	16.4 %	16.6 %	18.4 %
Violent	8.0	9.8	14.8
Property	26.9	30.3	10.6
Drugs	24.8	26.4	25.3
Public-order	5.2	6.9	6.8

- For experts in the field of crime, violence, and drug abuse, there is no doubt that there is a connection between drug use and violence. As Joseph A. Califano, Jr., of the National Center on Addiction and Substance Abuse at Columbia University and the former Secretary of Health, Education, and Welfare stated, "Drugs like marijuana, heroin and cocaine are not dangerous because they are illegal; they are illegal because they are dangerous."[208] Drug use is not a victimless crime. If you really want to hear the truth about drug use and subsequent behavior, or the arguments of legalizing a specific drug, go talk with a victim of a drug-related crime.

Fact 8: Alcohol and tobacco have caused significant health, social, and crime problems in this country, and legalized drugs would only make the situation worse.

- The "legalization lobby" claims that drugs are no more dangerous than alcohol, and no more harmful than smoking cigarettes. However, drunk driving remains one of the primary ways Americans die. Do we want our bus drivers, nurses, and airline pilots to be able to take drugs one evening, and operate freely at work the next day? Do we want to add to the destruction by making "drugged driving" vastly more common than it already is?

- Drugs are far more addictive than alcohol. According to Dr. Mitchell Rosenthal, director of Phoenix House, only 10 percent of drinkers become alcoholics, while up to 75 percent of regular illicit drug users become addicted.

- Even accepting, for the sake of argument, the legalization analogy, alcohol use in the United States has taken a tremendous physical and social toll on Americans. Legalization proponents would have the problems multiplied by greatly adding to the class of drug-addicted Americans. To put it in perspective, less than 8 percent of the population uses illegal drugs of any kind regularly. That's 20 million users of all illegal drugs, compared to 71 million tobacco users, and over 129 million alcohol users.[209]

- According to the Centers for Disease Control and Prevention, during 2005 there were 33,541 drug-induced deaths; and 21,634 alcohol-induced deaths (excluding accidents and homicides). [210] We all pay a high price for drug use – not only in lives lost, but in social costs. The Office of National Drug Control Policy estimates that for the year 2002, societal costs associated with drug use in the United States were $180 billion.[211] Legalization of drugs would compound the problems in the already overburdened health care, social service, and criminal justice systems. And it would demand a staggering new tax burden on the public to pay for the costs.

- Drug-impaired driving is also a problem. In 2007, nearly 10 million people reported driving under the influence of illicit drugs in the past year. 213 According to the National Highway Transportation Safety Administration, drugs -- often in combination with alcohol are used by approximately 10 to 22 percent of drivers involved in car accidents.214

- If drugs were widely available under legalization, they would no doubt be easily obtained by young people, despite age restrictions. According to the 2008 National Survey on Drug Use and Health, more than half (129 million) of Americans aged 12 or older were current drinkers, while an estimated 20 million or (8 percent) were current illicit drug users.[215]

- If private companies were to handle distribution—as is done with alcohol—the American consumer could expect a blizzard of profit-driven advertising encouraging drug use, just as we now face with alcohol advertising. If the government were to distribute drugs, either the taxpayer would have to pay for its production and distribution, or the government would be forced to market the drugs to earn the funds necessary to stay in business. Furthermore, the very act of official government distribution of drugs would send the wrong message that drug use is safe.

Prohibition

- Claims that prohibition didn't work overlook the fact that most historians agree that national prohibition succeeded both in lowering consumption and in retaining political support until the onset of the Great Depression radically changed voters priorities. Repeal resulted more from this contextual shift than from characteristics of prohibition itself.

- One favorite argument of those who claim prohibition didn't work point to the growth of organized crime. Although organized crime flourished under its sway, historians trace the beginnings of organized crime in the United States to the mid to late-1800s. Organized crime existed before prohibition was enacted, and persisted long after its repeal.

- The laws developed after 1919 by the 18th Amendment and the Volstead Act, which charged the Treasury Department with enforcement of the new restrictions, was far from all-embracing. The amendment prohibited the commercial manufacture and distribution of alcoholic beverages; it did not prohibit use, nor production for one's own consumption.

- Alcohol consumption declined dramatically during prohibition. Cirrhosis death rates for men were 29.5 per 100,000 in 1911 and 10.7 in 1929. Admissions to state mental hospitals for alcoholic psychosis declined from 10.1 per 100,000 in 1919 to 4.7 in 1928.

- Arrests for public drunkenness and disorderly conduct declined 50 percent between 1916 and 1922. For the population as a whole, the best estimates are that consumption of alcohol declined by 30 percent to 50 percent. Violent crime did not increase dramatically during prohibition. Homicide rates rose dramatically from 1900 to 1910, but remained roughly constant during prohibition's 14 year rule. Organized crime may have become more visible and lurid during prohibition, but it existed before and after.

- Following the repeal of prohibition, alcohol consumption increased. Prohibition did not end alcohol use, but it did succeeded in reducing, by one-third, the consumption of a product that had wide historical and popular sanction.

- It's wrong to draw a parallel between alcohol prohibition in the 1920's and the current status of marijuana, heroin, and other dangerous drugs. The 18th Amendment took a popular activity, alcohol sales, which was widely tolerated, and made it illegal. It did so after more than a century of growing concern over the effects that excessive alcohol consumption was having on society. In contrast, the use of marijuana, heroin, or other controlled drugs has never been a widely accepted activity.

- In addition, the idealistic goals of prohibition went beyond what many initial supporters of prohibition thought they were supporting, and lacked flexibility that would allow policy adjustments. In contrast, our nation's current drug laws are built upon the Controlled Substances Act, which contains a series of increasingly restrictive schedules that allow for the appropriate regulation of various drugs, as well as a mechanism to move substances from one regulatory status to another.

- A democratic society may decide that recreational drinking is worth the price in traffic fatalities and other consequences. But the common claim that laws backed by morally motivated political movements cannot reduce drug use is wrong.

- Not only are the facts of prohibition misunderstood, but the lessons are misapplied to the current situation. Legalizing drug use will launch us into a new drug epidemic.

- The real lesson of prohibition is that the society can make a dent in the consumption of drugs through laws. There is a price to be paid for such restrictions, of course. But for drugs such as heroin and cocaine, which are dangerous but currently largely unpopular, that price is small relative to the benefits.

- There is no uniform drug policy in Europe. Some countries have liberalized their laws, while others have instituted strict drug control policies, which means that the so-called "European Model" is a misnomer. Like America, the various countries of Europe are looking for new ways to combat the worldwide problem of drug abuse.

Fact 9: Europe's more liberal drug policies are not the right model for America.

- Over the past decade, European drug policy has gone through some dramatic changes toward greater liberalization. The Netherlands, considered to have led the way in the liberalization of drug policy, is only one of a number of Western European countries to relax penalties for marijuana possession. Now several European nations are looking to relax penalties on all drugs—including cocaine and heroin—as Portugal did in July 2001, when minor possession of all drugs was decriminalized (not legalized).

- In recent years the European Monitoring Centre for Drugs and Drug Addiction (EMCDDA) has reported a tendency among European countries to make a stronger distinction in their drug laws between those who use drugs and those who sell or traffic drugs. This distinction is reflected in the reduction of penalties for drug use in some countries, though others have not changed or increased penalties.[216]

- EMCDDA reports that recently, the penalties for drug offenses in Europe have generally increased. "Most of the reported drug law offenses are related to use and possession for use rather than supply, and whereas offenses related to supply have increased by 12 percent, those related to possession have increased by over 50 percent." Cannabis continues to be the drug most often associated with drug law offenses in Europe.[217]

- While cannabis remains the number one drug of choice in Europe, and cocaine use on the rise, heroin remains the most serious public health issue and accounts for a large proportion of the overall health and social costs associated with drug use.[218] Increased cocaine and heroin use are not the policy outcomes of an effective drug strategy.

- The United Kingdom has also experimented with the relaxation of drug laws. Until the mid-1960s, British physicians were allowed to prescribe heroin to certain classes of addicts. According to political scientist James Q. Wilson, "a youthful drug culture emerged with a demand for drugs far different from that of the older addicts." Many addicts chose to boycott the program and continued to get their heroin from illicit drug distributors. The British Government's experiment with controlled heroin distribution, says Wilson, resulted in, at a minimum, a 30-fold increase in the number of addicts in 10 years.

- A major newspaper in England, The Independent, reversed its very public stance in support of marijuana. After a pro-cannabis editorial appeared in 1997, 16,000 people marched on London's Hyde Park. The editorial and a subsequent march were credited with forcing the government to downgrade the legal status of cannabis to Class C. However, an editorial in the March 18, 2007 issue, titled "Cannabis: An Apology," states that the paper is reversing its decision. "In 1997, when this paper called for decriminalization, 1,600 people were being treated for cannabis addiction. Today, the number is 22,000." Concerns such as the record number of teenagers requiring drug treatment as a result of smoking 'skunk' (a highly potent cannabis strain), and the growing proof that skunk causes mental illnesses were cited among the reasons for this reversal.[227]

- In a statement to the press, British Home Secretary Jacqui Smith announced on May 8, 2008, that cannabis is being reclassified back to a Class B drug, sending a strong message that the drug is harmful. Addressing the House of Commons, Secretary Smith cited the need to update public policies to match recent scientific evidence about the serious harms of marijuana use, "the enforcement response must reflect the danger that the drug poses to individuals, and in turn, to communities."[228] This reclassification went into effect in January, 2009.[229]

- Liberalization of marijuana laws in Switzerland has likewise produced damaging results. After liberalization, Switzerland became a magnet for drug users from many other countries. In 1987, Zurich permitted drug use and sales in a part of Platzpitz, dubbed "Needle Park." By 1992, the number of regular drug users at the park reportedly swelled from a few hundred at the outset in 1987 to about 20,000. The area around the park became crime-ridden, forcing closure of the park. The experiment has since been terminated.[230]

- High levels of alcohol and drug consumption by young people in Europe is leading to an increase in unsafe sexual practices and a consequent rise in sexually-transmitted disease infections according to a recently published study by the European Institute of Studies on Prevention.[231]

- According to the latest report on the state of the drug problem in Europe published by the European Monitoring Committee on Drugs and Drug Addiction, cocaine use is continuing to rise. The report highlights the need for vigilance in response to changes in the opiate problem. It records that there are between 1.3 and 1.7 million problem opiate (mainly heroin) users throughout the EU and Norway, and points out that heroin accounts for Europe's largest drug-related health and social costs.[232] The United States has dealt with increases in cocaine use and reversed the trend. Rather than point to Europe's more liberal drug policies as an example for United States drug policy, perhaps there are effective lessons that Europe could learn from America's experience.

The Netherlands Experience

- The Netherlands has led Europe in the liberalization of drug policy. "Coffee shops" began to emerge throughout the Netherlands in 1976, offering marijuana products for sale. Possession and sale of marijuana are not legal, but coffee shops are permitted to operate and sell marijuana under certain restrictions, including a limit of no more than 5 grams sold to a person at any one time, no alcohol or hard drugs, no minors, and no advertising. In the Netherlands, it is illegal to sell or possess marijuana products. So coffee shop operators must purchase their marijuana products from illegal drug trafficking organizations.

o Many Dutch communities are struggling with how to address the increased crime and other negative consequences associated with their drug policies. For example, according to a *New York Times* article, "The mayor (of Maastricht) wants to move most of the city's 16 licensed cannabis clubs to the edge of town, preferably close to the border (with Belgium and Germany)...Mayor Gerd Leers is reacting to growing concerns among residents who "complain of traffic problems, petty crime, loitering and public urination. There have been shootings between Balkan gangs. Maastricht's small police force...is already spending one-third of its time on drug-related problems." Cannabis clubs have drawn "pushers of hard drugs from Amsterdam, who often harass people on the streets." The clubs have also attracted people looking to buy marijuana in quantity. Piet Tans, a police spokesman also stated that "people who come from far away don't just come for the five grams you can buy legally over the counter...they think pounds and kilos; they go to the dealers who operate in the shadows."[219]

o Moving the clubs did not prove to be an effective strategy to deal with the problem. As of January 1, 2010, coffee shops in the province of Limburg (which includes Maastricht) will be accessible only to registered members. Justice Minister Ernst Hirsch Ballin also stated that "it would become easier to keep minors out of the coffee shops."[220]

o The growing use of marijuana is responsible for more than increased crime. It has widespread social implications as well. The head of Holland's best-known drug abuse rehabilitation center has described what the new drug culture has created: The strong form of marijuana that most of the young people smoke, he says, produces "...a chronically passive individual—someone who is lazy, who doesn't want to take initiatives, doesn't want to be active—the kid who'd prefer to lie in bed with a joint in the morning rather than getting up and doing something."[221]

o Recognizing that the government needs to take firm action to deal with the increasing levels of addiction, in April 2001 the Dutch government established the Penal Care Facility for Addicts. Like American Drug Treatment Courts, this facility is designed to detain and treat addicts (of any drug) who repeatedly commit crimes and have failed voluntary treatment facilities. Offenders may be held in this facility for up to two years, during which time they will go through a three-phase program. The first phase focuses on detoxification, while the second and third phases focus on training for social reintegration.

o   Due to international pressure on permissive Dutch cannabis policy and domestic complaints over the spread of marijuana "coffee shops," the Netherlands has reconsidered its legalization measures. After marijuana became normalized, consumption nearly tripled – from 15 percent to 44 percent – among 18 to 20 year-old Dutch youth.[222] As a result of stricter local government policies, the number of cannabis "coffeehouses" in the Netherlands was reduced – from 1,179 in 1997 to 737 in 2004, a 37-percent decrease in seven years.[223]

o   On January 2, 2007, the majority of the City Council in Amsterdam voted in favor of introducing a city-wide ban on smoking marijuana in public in areas where young people smoking joints had been a public nuisance. Their decision was based upon the success of the experimental ban in the city of DeBaarsjes.[224]

o   "Contrary to what is often claimed by supporters of the tolerant Dutch drug policy, cannabis usage by young people in the Netherlands is not lower, but actually higher than average in Europe," according to the 2007 European School Survey on Alcohol and Other Drugs (ESPAD). "Over one-quarter (28 percent) of Dutch youngsters aged 15 and 16 surveyed said they have used cannabis sometime in their life, compared with an average of 19 percent in Europe. Current cannabis usage (at least once in the month prior to the survey) is more than double the European average in the Netherlands (15 percent versus 7 percent)."[225]

o   An article published in the Netherlands in April 2009 summarizes the challenge now faced by the Dutch as a result of their drug policies. "The Netherlands has risen in the ranking order of 35 European countries from number 12 in 2003 to number five on recent cannabis usage. . . .Dutch youngsters, possibly due to the liberal climate, widely believe that cannabis is innocent and the proportion of school children that think regular cannabis usage involves big risks is the lowest in the Netherlands (50 percent) of all countries surveyed." [226]

Fact 10: Most non-violent drug users get treatment, not jail time.

- There is a popular belief that America's prisons are filling up with drug users arrested for simple possession of marijuana. This is a myth. In reality, a vast majority of inmates in state and federal prison for marijuana have been found guilty of much more than simple possession, and many of those serving time for marijuana possession pled down to possession in order to avoid prosecution on much more serious charges.

- The Bureau of Justice Statistics (BJS) divided drug offenders in state prison systems into two general categories: trafficking offenses, which accounted for 70 percent of drug law violators, and possession offenses, accounting for about 27 percent.[234] Out of the total number of state inmates doing time for any drug offense, 83 percent had a prior criminal history. In other words, the large majority were not first time offenders. They were people who had committed crimes in the past, and nearly two-thirds of them (62 percent) had multiple prior convictions.[235] Marijuana accounted for just 13 percent of all state drug offenders.[236]

- An examination of the data from the broader perspective of the entire prison population, the data shows that in 1997 marijuana was involved in the conviction of only 2.7 percent of all state inmates. About 1.6 percent of the state prison populations were held for offenses involving just marijuana, while just 0.7 percent were incarcerated with marijuana possession as the only charge.[237]

Figure 2 Inmates in state prison for marijuana offenses (1997)[238]

```
Drug Possession Offenses_____ 5.6% of all state inmates
First-time drug offenders _____ 3.6% of all state inmates
Offenses involving marijuana_____ 2.7% of all state inmates
Prisoners held for marijuana only_____ 1.6% of all state inmates
Prisoners held for marijuana possession only   0.7% of all state inmates
First time offenders held only for
marijuana possession (any amount)_____ 0.3% of all state inmates
```

- If you exclude prisoners with criminal histories, only 0.3 percent of all state inmates were first time marijuana possession offenders (see Figure 2). This statistic refers to possession of any amount—even as much as a hundred pounds or more—not just "personal use" quantities. Of the more than 1.2 million people serving time in state prisons across America, only 3,600 individuals were sentenced on a first offense for possession of marijuana. Again, this figure includes possession of <u>any</u> amount.[239]

- The numbers at the federal level tell a similar story. Out of all drug defendants sentenced in federal court for marijuana crimes in 2001, the overwhelming majority were convicted for trafficking. Only 2.3 percent (186 people) received sentences for simple possession. Of the 174 for whom sentencing is known, only 63 actually spent time behind bars.[240]

- In the same 1997 review that looked at state prisoners, BJS found that drug possession offenders made up 18.3 percent of the federal inmate population. BJS researchers calculated that 11.9 percent of all federal prisoners in 1997 were serving time on charges that included some kind of marijuana violation, and that 9.3 percent were being held only for marijuana offenses.

- If traffickers and repeat offenders were removed from the mix, these numbers drop even further. Only 2.2 percent of federal inmates in 1997 had been sentenced just on charges of marijuana possession and less than half of that group—only one percent—were first time offenders.[241]

- Current data from the United States Sentencing Commission (USSC) reinforces the BJS findings. In 2008, according to the USSC, 25,337 people were sentenced in federal court for drug crimes under six offense categories (see Figure 3). Marijuana accounted for 6,337 and (25.0 percent), and of the 6,337 people sentenced, only 99 people, or 1.6 percent, were sentenced for "simple possession" of marijuana. [242]

- In 1998, Columbia University's National Center on Addiction and Substance Abuse (CASA) published the results of a three-year study into drug and alcohol abuse/addiction among inmates in federal and state prisons and local jails. In *Behind Bars: Substance Abuse and America's Prison Population*, which used information collected by BJS and other sources, CASA stated that, based on the available data, "it appears that few inmates could be in prison or jail solely for possession of small amounts of marijuana and the number is likely so small that it would have little or no impact on overcrowding or the vast gap between the need for treatment and training and available slots."[243]

Policy Shift to Treatment

- For those who end up hooked on drugs, there are also programs, like drug courts, that offer non-violent users the option of seeking treatment and staying out of either federal or state prisons. Drug court programs provide court supervision, unlike voluntary treatment centers. These courts are given a special responsibility to handle cases involving drug-addicted offenders through an extensive supervision and treatment program.

- As an alternative to less effective interventions, drug courts quickly identify substance-abusing offenders, and place them under strict court monitoring and community supervision, coupled with effective, long-term treatment services. Drug courts represent the coordinated efforts of the judiciary, prosecution, defense, probation, law enforcement, mental health, social service, and treatment communities to actively and forcefully intervene and break the cycle of substance abuse, addiction, and crime. [245]

- Drug court programs use the varied experiences and skills of a wide variety of law enforcement and treatment professionals: judges, prosecutors, defense counsels, substance abuse treatment specialists, probation officers, law enforcement and correctional personnel, educational and vocational experts, community leaders, and others — all focused on one goal: to help cure addicts of their addiction, and to keep them cured.

- Nationwide, 75 percent of drug court graduates remain arrest-free at least two years after leaving the program.[246]

- A 2000 Vera Institute of Justice report concluded that "the body of literature on recidivism is now strong enough, despite lingering methodological weaknesses, to conclude that completing a drug court program reduces the likelihood of future arrest."[247]

- In a February 2005 report, the Government Accountability Office concluded that adult drug court programs substantially reduce crime by lowering re-arrest and conviction rates among drug court graduates well after program's completion, providing overall greater cost/benefits for the drug court participants and graduates than comparison group members.

- Drug courts now exist in a growing number of jurisdictions: e.g., Australia and Canada (1999); Ireland (2000); Bermuda, Brazil, Cayman Islands, Jamaica, and Scotland (2001); New Zealand, Mauritius, England, Wales, Northern Ireland (2002).

Figure 3 Primary Drug Type of Offenders Sentenced Under Each Drug Guideline (FY 2008)[244]

DRUG TYPE	TOTAL	Drug Trafficking N	%	Protected Locations N	%	Contiuing Criminal Enterprise N	%	Communication Facility N	%	Rent/Manage Drug Establishment N	%	Simple Possesion N	%
Total	25,337	24,605	97.1%	348	1.4%	18	0.1%	0	0.0%	88	0.3%	2	1.1%
Powder Cocaine	5,889	5,769	98.0%	68	1.2%	6	0.1%	0	0.0%	14	0.2%	3	0.5%
Crack Cocaine	6,168	5,913	95.9%	188	3.0%	1	0.0%	0	0.0%	38	0.6%	28	0.5%
Heroin	1,476	1,436	97.3%	26	1.8%	1	0.1%	0	0.0%	1	0.1%	12	0.8%
Marijuana	6,337	6,196	97.8%	27	0.4%	2	0.0%	0	0.0%	13	0.2%	99	1.6%
Methamphetamine	4,347	4,238	97.5%	24	0.6%	6	0.1%	0	0.0%	18	0.4%	61	1.4%
Other	1,120	1,053	94.0%	15	1.3%	2	0.2%	0	0.0%	4	0.4%	46	4.1%

- Drug courts reflect a transformation of the way courts have traditionally dealt with drug-abusing offender criminal casework. The traditional process was adversarial, emphasized the efficient but backward-looking adjudication of claims, rights and responsibilities, and involved few participants and stakeholders. The transformed process practiced in drug courts is collaborative, needs-based, and emphasizes forward-looking, post-adjudication problem-solving, and dispute avoidance, with a wide range of participants and stakeholders. It is aimed at efficient case processing and effective case outcomes to stop criminal recidivism and drug abuse.

- When drug abuse prevention fails, the public pays a high price, particularly if abusers commit serious offences under the influence of drugs (e.g., domestic violence), or commit crimes to help pay for their habit (e.g., burglary, theft).[248]

- The largest statewide study on drug courts to date was released in 2003 by the Center for Court Innovation (CCI). The study analyzed the impact of New York State's Drug Court system. The study found that the re-conviction rate among 2,135 defendants who participated in six of the state's drug courts was, on average, sinificanatly lower (13 percent to 47 percent) over three years than the for the same types of offenders who did not enter the drug court. The study also concluded that drug court cases reached initial disposition more quickly than conventional court cases and that the statewide drug court retention rate was approximately 65 percent, exceeding the national average of 60 percent.[249]

- Nonviolent drug offenders in drug courts in St. Louis, Missouri who were placed in treatment instead of prison generally earned more money and took less from the welfare system than those who successfully completed probation. The study compared the 219 individuals who were the program's first graduates in 2001 with 219 people who pleaded guilty to drug charges during the same period and completed probation. For each drug court graduate, the cost to taxpayers was $7,793, which was $1,449 more than those on probation. However, during the two years following program completion, each graduate cost the city $2,615 less than those on probation. The savings were realized in higher wages and related taxes paid, as well as lower costs for health care and mental health services.[250]

- Drug courts save taxpayers money. The Urban Institute estimates a favorable cost/benefit ration as high as $3.36 for every $1.00 invested in treating drug-addicted offenders in drug courts. [251]

Notes

1. "National Drug Threat Assessment," December 2009, page III.

2. Marin Institute Fact Sheet, "The Costs of Alcohol," June 24, 2008.

3. As of April 1, 2009.

4. See: http://www.CDC.gov/tobacco.

5. Heron, et al, "Deaths: Final Data for 2006," U.S. Dept of Health and Human Services, Centers for Disease Control and Prevention, National Vital Statistics Reports, Vol. 57, Number 14, April 2009, DHHS Pub No (PAS) 2009-1120 (Tables 21 and 22), see: http://www.cdc.gov/nchs/data/nvsr/nvsr57/nvsr57_14.pdf.

6. INTRAVAL Bureau for Research and Consistency, "Coffeeshops in the Netherlands 2004," Dutch Ministry of Justice, June 2005, http://www.intraval.nl/en/b/b45_html.

7. See: 21 U.S.C. § 881.

8. 21 U.S.C. § 811(h).

9. See: McCullough v. Maryland, 17 U.S. 316 (1819); see also U.S. v. Cal. State Bd. of Equalization, 650 F.2d 1127 (9th Cir. 1981), 456 U.S. 901 (1982), aff'd, 456 U.S. 985 (1982), reh'g denied.

10. See, e g.: U.S. v. $20,193.39 U.S. Currency, 16 F.3d 344, 346 (9th Cir. 1994).

11. See, e.g.: 18 U.S.C. § 983(d)(3) and 21 U.S.C. § 853(n)(6)(B).

12. 21 U.S.C. § 812(c), Schedule I(c)(10).

13. See 66 Fed. Reg. 20038, 20050-52 (2001) (DEA denial of petition to remove marijuana from schedule I based on FDA scientific and medical evaluation), pet. for review dismissed, Gettman v. DEA, 290 F.3d 430 (D.C. Cir. 2002).

14. U.S. v. Oakland Cannabis Buyers' Cooperative 532 U.S. 483, 491, 494 & n.7 (2001).

15. 532 U.S. 483 (2001).

16. Gonzales v. Raich, 545 U.S. 1 (2005).

17. The main drug control treaties currently in force to which the United States is signatory are: The Single Convention on Narcotic Drugs, 1961, 18 U.S.T. 1407; The Convention on Psychotropic Substances, 1971, 32 U.S.T. 543; and the Convention Against Illicit Traffic in Narcotic Drugs and Psychotropic Substances, 1988, 28 I.LM. 493. Among the United States obligations pursuant to these treaties are: (i) To enact and carry out legislation disallowing the use of Schedule I drugs outside of authorized research; (ii) To make it a criminal offense, subject to imprisonment, to traffic in illicit drugs or to aid and abet such trafficking; and (iii) To prohibit the cultivation of marijuana except by persons licensed by, and under the direct supervision of, the federal Government.

18. U.N. International Narcotics Control Board, United Nations, "Report 1998" at par. 259, U.N. Sales No. E.99.XI.1, http://www.incb.org/incb/en/annual_report_1998.html.

19. 545 U.S. at 27-28.

20. 545 U.S. at 22

21. See 21 U.S.C. § 881.

22. 21 U.S.C. § 811(h).

23. See: McCullough v. Maryland, 17 U.S. 316 (1819); see also U.S. v. Cal. State Bd. of Equalization, 650 F.2d 1127 (9th Cir. 1981), 456 U.S. 901 (1982), affirmed, 456 U.S. 985 (1982), registration denied.

24. See, e g., U.S. v. $20,193.39 U.S. Currency, 16 F.3d 344, 346 (9th Cir. 1994).

25. See, e.g., 18 U.S.C. § 983(d)(3) and 21 U.S.C. § 853(n)(6)(B).

26. Moore, Mark H., "Actually, Prohibition Was a Success," Harvard's Kennedy School of Government, October 16, 1989.

27. National Drug Control Strategy, Office of National Drug Control Policy, "2009 Annual Report," January 2009, page 1; and National Institute for Drug Abuse and the University of Michigan, Monitoring the Future, December 11, 2008.

28. Johnson, L.D., O'Malley, P.M., Bachman, J.G., and Schulenberg, J.E. "Teen marijuana use tilts up, while some drugs decline in use." University of Michigan Press Release, Monitoring the Future 2009, www.monitoringthefuture.org.

29. National Drug Control Strategy, Office of National Drug Control Policy, "2009 Annual Report," January 2009, page 1.

30. Department of Health and Human Services, Substance Abuse and Mental Health Services Administration,Office of Applied Studies, "Results from the 2008 National Survey on Drug Use and Health, National Findings," September 2009, page 1.

31. DEA STRIDE (System to Retrieve Information on Drug Evidence) data, January 2009.

32. Serious Organised Crime Agency, "Annual Report 2008/09," May 2009, page 40.

33. Department of Health and Human Services, Substance Abuse and Mental Health Services Administration, Office of Applied Studies, "Results from the 2007 National Survey on Drug Use and Health," September 2008, page 1.

34. National Drug Control Strategy, Office of National Drug Control Policy, "2009 Annual Report," January 2009, page 2.

35. Department of Health and Human Services, Substance Abuse and Mental Health Services Administration,Office of Applied Studies, "Results from the 2008 National Survey on Drug Use and Health, National Findings," September 2008, page 1.

36. Ibid. Page 1.

37. "CORK Bibliography: Adolescents-Initiation of Alcohol and Drug Use," December 2008, www.projectcork.org/ bibliographies/data/Bibliography_Adolescents_Initiation%20of%20Alcohol_and_Drug_Use.html. Last accessed September 22, 2009.

38. National Drug Control Strategy, Office of National Drug Control Policy, "2009 Annual Report," January 2009.

39. National Institute on Drug Abuse, "Principles of Drug Addiction Treatment, A Research-Based Guide," Secon Edition, April 2009, page 13.

40. Roman et al, the Urban Institute and Caliber, "Recidivism Rates for Drug Court Graduates: Nationally Based Estimate – Final Report," Washington D.C., 2003.

41. Fluellen, R. and Trone, J, Vera Institute of Justice, "Issues in Brief: Do Drug Courts Save Jail and Prison Beds?" New York, NY, May 2000.

42. Rempel, M., Fox-Kralstein, D., Cissner, A., Cohoen, R., Labriola, M., Farole, D., Bader, A., and Magnani, M., "The New York State Adult Drug Court Evaluation: Policies, Participants, and Impacts," 2003.

43. Institute for Applied Research, "A Cost-Benefit Analysis of the Saint Louis City Adult Felony Drug Court," St. Louis, MO, 2004.

44. The Urban Institute, "To Treat or Not to Treat: Evidence on the Prospects of Expanding treatment for Drug-Involved Offenders," 2008.

45. Pacula, R., Grossman, M., Chaloupka, F., O'Malley, P., Johnston, L., and Farrelly, M., "Marijuana and Youth," October 2000.

46. Department of Health and Human Services, Substance Abuse and Mental Health Services Administration, Office of Applied Studies, "Results from the 2008 National Survey on Drug Use and Health: National Findings," September 2009.

47. Pacula, Rosalie Liccardo, National Bureau of Economic Research, "Marijuana Use and Policy: What We Know and Have Yet to Learn," Winter 2005, http://www.nber.org/reporter/winter05/pacula.html.

48. Department of Health and Human Services, Substance Abuse and Mental Health Services .Health, National Findings," September 2009.

49. In addition to the CSA and FDCA, marketing products in such a manner raises potential trademark infringement issues. Letter of response to the Honorable John Conyers, Jr., Chairman of the Committee on the Judiciary, U.S. House of Representatives, on enforcement of federal laws with respect to marijuana traffickers in California, from Keith B. Nelson, Principal Deputy Assistant Attorney General, July 25, 2008.

50. Ibid.

51. DEA press release, "Designer Cocaine-Candy Flavored Drug Seized in Undercover Investigation: Flavors Include Strawberry, Lemon, Coconut and Cinnamon." See: http://webster/dea/pubs/states/newsrel/sanfran031008.html, March 10, 2008. Also, DEA press release, "'Pot Tarts' and 'Buddafingers' Manufacturers Busted: DEA arrests 12, seizes marijuana-laced candy and soft drinks in San Francisco Bay Area,"see http://webster/dea/pubs/states/newsrel/sanfran031606.html, March 16, 2006.

52. See: http://www.justthinktwice.com/hot/cheese.cfm.

53. "Teen Methamphetamine Use, Cigarette Smoking at Lowest Levels in NIIDA's 2009 Monitoring the Future Survey," Press Release, National Institutes of Health, National Institute on Drug Abuse, December 14, 2009 p 2.

54. U.S. Department of Health and Human Services, Centers for Disease Control and Prevention, "Unintentional Poisoning Deaths – United States, 1999-2004," released February 9, 2007, 56(05); 93-96, see: http://www.cdc.gov/mmwr/preview/mmwrhtml/mm5605a1.htm.

55. Ibid.

56. Heron et al, "Deaths: Final Data for 2006," U.S. Dept of Health and Human Services, Centers for Disease Control and Prevention, National Vital Statistics Reports, Vol. 57, Number 14, April 2009, DHHS Pub No (PAS) 2009-1120 (Tables 21 and 22), see: http://www.cdc.gov/nchs/data/nvsr/nvsr57/nvsr57_14.pdf.

57. U.S. Department of Health and Human Services, Substance Abuse and Mental Health Administration, Office of Applied Studies, "Results from the 2006 National Survey on Drug Use and Health: National Findings," September 2007, pages 2-3.

58. U.S. Department of Health and Human Services, National Institutes of Health, National Institute on Drug Abuse, "Research Report - Cocaine Abuse and Addiction," www.nida.nih/gov/researchreports/cocaine/cocaine.html.

59. Department of Justice, Drug Enforcement Administration, Office of Diversion Control, www.deadiversion.usdoj.gov/drugs_concern/cocaine.htm.

60. U.S. Department of Health and Human Services, National Institutes of Health, National Institute on Drug Abuse, "Research Report - Cocaine Abuse and Addiction." www.nida.nih/gov/researchreports/cocaine/cocaine.html.

61. Ibid.

62. Ibid.

63. Ibid.

64. Ibid.

65. U.S. Department of Health and Human Services, Substance Abuse and Mental Health Services Administration, Office of Applied Studies, "Results from the 2007 National Survey on Drug Use and Health: National Findings," September 2009.

66. Johnston, L.D., O'Malley, P. M., Bachman, J. G., and Schulenberg, J. E., Unversity of Michigan, December 14, 2009, www.monitoringthefuture.org. "Teen marijuana use tilts up, while some drugs decline."

67. A drug-related Emergency Department (ED) visit is any ED visit related to recent drug use. This is the definition of a DAWN case effective January 1, 2003. To be a DAWN case, a drug needs only to be implicated in the visit; the drug does not have to have caused the visit. One patient may make repeated visits to an ED or to several EDs, thus producing a number of visits. The number of unique patients involved in the reported drug-related ED visits cannot be estimated, because no direct patient identifiers are collected by DAWN. U.S. Department of Health and Human Services, Substance Abuse and Mental Health Services Administration, "Drug Abuse Warning Network, 2006: National Estimates of Drug-Related Emergency Department Visits," Appendix B, Glossary of Terms, August 2008.

68. National Institutes of Health, National Institute on Drug Abuse, "Research Report: Heroin Abuse and Addiction," May 2005.

69. Department of Justice, Drug Enforcement Administration, "Drugs of Abuse," 2005.

70. National Institutes of Health, National Institute on Drug Abuse, "Research Report: Heroin Abuse and Addiction," May 2005.

71. Partnership for a Drug-Free America, Heroin Addiction, Effects of Heroin, Heroin Facts, http://www.drugfree.org.

72. National Institutes of Health, National Institute on Drug Abuse, "InfoFacts: Heroin," May 2006.

73. Ibid.

74. Johnston, L.D., O'Malley, P. M., Bachman, J. G., and Schulenberg, J. E., Unversity of Michigan, December 14, 2009, www.monitoringthefuture.org. "Teen marijuana use tilts up, while some drugs decline. U.S. Department of Health and Human Services, National Institutes of Health, National Institute for Drug Abuse.

75. U.S. Department of Health and Human Services, Substance Abuse and Mental Health Administration, "Results From the 2008 National Survey on Drug Use and Health: National Findings," September 2009.

76. U.S. Department of Health and Human Services, Substance Abuse and Mental Health Administration, "Drug Abuse Warning Network, 2006: National Estimates of Drug-Related Emergency Department Visits," August 2008.

77. "Marijuana and Heart Attacks," Washington Post, 3 March 2000.

78. "One cannabis joint as bad as five cigarettes," Reuters, 31 July 2007. See: http://www.reuters.com/article/healthNews/idUSL3173105820070731.

79. Office of National Drug Control Policy press release, " Increased Potency of Smoked Marijuana May Be Responsible for Serious Mental Health Consequences in Teens," June 12, 2008, and "New Report Finds Highest Levels of THC in U.S. Marijuana to Date," May 14, 2009.

80. I.B. Adams and B.R. Martin, "Cannabis Pharmacology and Toxicology in Animals and Humans," Addiction Journal, 91: 1585-1614, 1996.

81. U.S. Department of Health and Human Services, National Institutes of Health, National Institute on Drug Abuse, "Smoking Any Substance Raises Risk of Lung Infections," NIDA Notes, Volume 12, Number 1, January/February 1997.

82. Tetrault, Jeannette M., MD, et al, "Effects of Marijuana Smoking on Pulmonary Function Respiratory Complications: A Systematic Review," Archives of Internal Medicine, 167:221-228, 2007; Science Daily, "Long-term Marijuana Smoking Leads to Respiratory Complaints, see: www.sceincedaily.com/releases/200702/070212184119.htm.

83. "Recommendations Regarding the Use of Cannabis in Multiple Sclerosis," National Clinical Advisory Board of the National Multiple Sclerosis Society, April 2, 2008.

84. U.S. Department of Health and Human Services, National Institutes of Health, National Institute on Drug Abuse, "Research Report: Marijuana Abuse," July 2005.

85. Ibid.

86. Ibid.

87. Ibid.

88. U.S. Department of Health and Human Services, National Institutes of Mental Health, National Institute on Drug Abuse, "Research Report: Marijuana Abuse," October 2001.

89. Ibid.

90. American Medical Association, "Policy H-95.952: Medical Marijuana." See also American Medical Association, Featured Council on Scientific Affairs, "Medical Marijuana (A-01)," June 2001. In 2001, the AMA updated their policy regarding medical marijuana, reflecting the results of this study.

91. American Cancer Society, "Experts: Pot Smoking is Not Best Choice to Treat Chemo Side-Effects," May 22, 2001. See: HTTP://www.cancer.org/docroot/NWS/content/update/NWS_1_1xU_Experts_Pot_Smoking_Is_Not_Best_Choice_to_Teat_Chemo_Side_Effects.asp.

92. American Academy of Pediatrics Committee on Substance Abuse and Committee on Adolescence Policy Statement, "Legalization of Marijuana: Potential Impact on Youth," Pediatrics, Vol. 113, No. 6, June 2004: 1825-1826. See also Joffe, Alain, MD, MPH, and Yancy, Samuel, MD, "Legalization of Marijuana Potential Impact on Youth," Pediatrics, Vol. 113, No.6, June 2004.

93. "Recommendations Regarding the Use of Cannabis in Multiple Sclerosis," National Clinical Advisory Board of the National Multiple Sclerosis Society, April 2, 2008.

94. "Australia: Doc Group Lobbies for Tougher Western Australia Marijuana Laws, Cites Mental Health Threat," The Western Australia, 24 May 2008. See: http://www.thewest.com/au/default.aspx?MenuID=158&ContentID=74974.

95. "Efforts to Counter the Trend Towards the Legalization of Drugs for Non-medical Use," United Nations Economic and Social Council, 44th plenary meeting, 22 July 2003.

96. International Narcotics Control Board press release, "INCB: U.S. Supreme Court Decision on Cannabis Upholds International Law," Professor Hamid Ghodse, INCB President, 8 June 2005.

97. "Doctors' Fears at Cannabis Change," BBC News, 21 January 2004.

98. Manchester Online. "Doctors Support Drive Against Cannabis," Manchester News, 21 January 2004, see: http://www.manchesteronline.co.uk/news/s/78/78826_doctors_support_drive_against_cannabis.html.

99. UK Home Office press release, "Government crackdown on cannabis," 7 May 2008, see: http://press.homeoffice.gov.uk/press-releases/government-crackdown-cannabis.

100. Ibid.

101. Ibid.

102. Goldschmidt, Lidush, Ph.D., et al, "Prenatal Marijuana Exposure and Intelligence Test Performance at Age 6," Journal of the American Academy of Child & Adolescent Psychiatry, 47(3):254-263, March 2008.

103. "A Functional MRI Study of the Effects of Cannabis on the Brain." Prof. Phillip McGuire, 2nd International Cannabis and Mental Health Conference, London, UK, May 1, 2007.

104. UPI.com, Science News, "Study: Marijuana may Affect Neuron Firing," November 29, 2006.

105. Laucius, Joanne, "Journal Articles Link Marijuana to Schizophrenia," August 28, 2006, see: www.Canada.com.

106. "Memory, Speed of Thinking and Other Cognitive Abilities Get Worse Over Time With Marijuana Use, " March 15, 2006, see: http://www.news-medical.net.

107. "Drug Abuse: Drug Czar, Others Warn Parents that Teen Marijuana Use Can Lead to Depression," Life Science Weekly, 31 May 2005.

108 Kearney, Simon, "Cannabis is Worst Drug for Psychosis," The Australian, 21 November 2005.

109. Curtis, John, "Study Suggests Marijuana Induces Temporary Schizophrenia-Like Effects," Yale Medicine, Fall/Winter 2004.

110. "Neurotoxicology: Neurocognitive Effects of Chronic Marijuana Use Characterized," Health & Medicine Week, 16 M ay 2005.

111. Robin Murray, "Teenage Schizophrenia is the Issue, Not Legality," Independent on Sunday, 18 March 2007, see: www.independent.co.uk.

112. Jonathan Owen, "UN Warns of Cannabis Dangers as it Backs 'IoS' Drugs 'Apology'," Independent on Sunday, 25 March 2007, see: www.independent.co.uk, and "Cannabis-related Schizophrenia Set to Rise, Say Researchers," Science Daily, 26 March 2007, see: www.sciencedaily.com/releases/2007/03/070324132832.htm.

113. "Marijuana Use Affects Blood Flow in Brain Even After Abstinence," Science Daily, 12 February 2005, see: www.sciencedaily.com/releases/2005/02/050211084701.htm; Neurology, 8 February 2005, 64.488-493.

114. "Marijuana Use Takes Toll on Adolescent Brain Function, Research Finds," Science Daily, 15 October 2008, see: http://www.scienedaily.com/releases/2008/10/081014111156.htm.

115. "Heavy Marijuana Use Linked to Gum Disease, Study Shows," Science Daily, 6 February 2008, see: http://www.sciencedaily.com/releases/2008/02/080205161239.htm; "Cannabis Smoking and Periodontal Disease Among Young Adults," The Journal of the American Medical Association, Vol. 299, No. 5, 6 February 2008, see: http://www.jama.ama-assn.org/cgi/content/full/299/5/25.

116. "Marijuana Smokers Face Rapid Lung Destruction – As Much As 20 Years Ahead of Tobacco Smokers." Science Daily, 27 January 2008, see: http://www.sciencedaily.com/releases/2008/01/080123104017.htm; and "Bullous Lung Disease Due to Marijuana," Respirology (2008) 13, 122-127.

117. "Marijuana Smoke Contains Higher Levels of Certain Toxins Than Tobacco Smoke," Science Daily, 18 December 2007, see: http://sciencedaily.com/releases/2007/12/071217110328.htm; and "A Comparison of Mainstream and Sidestream Marijuana and Tobacco Smoke Produced Under Two Machine Smoking Conditions," American Chemical Society, Chemical Research in Toxicology, 17 December 2008.

118. "Marijuana Worsens COPD Symptoms in Current Cigarette Smokers," American Thoracic Society, Science Daily, 23 May 2007.

119. "How Smoking Marijuana Damages the Fetal Brain," Karolinska Institute, Science Daily, 29 May 2007.

120. Martin Johnston, "Cannabis Linked to Lung Cancer Risk," New Zealand Herald, 27 March 2007.

121. "Marijuana Use Linked to Increased Risk of Testicular Cancer," Science Daily, 9 February 2009, see: http://www.scienedaily.com/releases/2009/02/090209075631.htm.

122. Baker, Toni, "Marijuana Use Linked to Bladder Cancer," January 26, 2006, see: http://www.medicalnewstoday.com.

123. "Marijuana Tied to Precancerous Lung Changes," Reuters, 13 July 2006, see: http://today.reuters.com/misc; see also: "The Association Between Marijuana Smoking and Lung Cancer," Archives of Internal Medicine, 10 July 2006, see: http://archinte.ama.assn.org/cgi/content/full/166/12/1359?maxtoshow.

124. "Cannabis More Toxic than Cigarettes: Study," French National Consumers' Institute, 60 Million Consumers April 2006, see: www.theage.com.au.

125. "Conception and Pregnancy Put at Risk by Marijuana Use," News-Medical.Net, 2 August 2006, see also: "Fatty Acid Amide Hydrolase Deficiency Limits Earl Pregnancy Events," Journal of Clinical Investigation research article, 22 March 2006, revised 23 May 2006, see: http://www.jci.org/cgi/content/full/116/8/2122.

126. "In Utero Marijuana Exposure Alters Infant Behavior," Reuters, 17 January 2007.

127. Tashkin, D.P., "Smoked Marijuana is a Cause of Lung Injury," Monaldi Archives for Chest Disease 63(2):93-100, 2005.

128. "Marijuana Associated with Same Respiratory Symptoms as Tobacco," YALE News Release, 13 January 2005, see: http://www.yale.edu/opa/newsr/05-01-13-01.all.htm; see also, "Marijuana Causes Same Respiratory Symptoms as Tobacco," 13 January 2005, 14WFIE.com.

129. News-Medical.Net, 24 May 2006.

130. See: http://www.nida.nih.gov/DirReports/DirRep207/DirectorReport8.html.

131. U.S. Department of Health and Human Services, Substance Abuse and Mental Health Services Administration, Office of Applied Studies, "Results from the 2007 National Survey on Drug Use and Health: National Findings." September 2008, page 1.

132. Office of National Drug Control Policy, "The Economic Cost of Drug Abuse in the United States, 1992-2002," December 2004, page vi.

133. U.S. Department of Health and Human Services, Centers for Disease Control and Prevention, "Unintentional Poisoning Deaths – United States, 1999-2004," released February 9, 2007, 56(05); 93-96, see: http://www.cdc.gov/mmwr/preview/mmwrhtml/mm5605a1.htm.

134. Heron, et al, "Deaths: Final Data for 2006," U.S. Department of Health and Human Services, Centers for Disease Control and Prevention, National Vital Statistics Reports, Vol. 57, Number 14, April 2009, DHHS Pub No. (PAS) 2009-1120 (Tables 21 and 22), see: http://www.cdc.gov/nchs/data/nvsr/nvsr57/nvsr57_14.pdf.

135. National Drug Control Strategy, Office of National Drug Control Policy, "2009 Annual Report," January 2009, page 12.

136. Heron, et al, "Deaths: Final Data for 2006," U.S. Department of Health and Human Services, Centers for Disease Control and Prevention, National Vital Statistics Reports, Vol. 57, Number 14, April 2009, DHHS Pub No (PAS) 2009-1120 (Tables 21 and 22), see: http://www.cdc.gov/nchs/data/nvsr/nvsr57/nvsr57_14.pdf.

137. U.S. Department of Health and Human Services, Substance Abuse and Mental Health Services Administration, Office of Applied Studies, "Drug Abuse Warning Network, 2006: National Estimates of Drug-Related Emergency. Department Visits," August 2008, page 7, see: http://DAWNinfo.samhsa.gov/.

138. University of Maryland, Center for Substance Abuse Research, CESAR FAX, Vol. 18, Issue 17, May 4, 2009, see: www.cesar.umd.edu.

139. HIV transmission Continues in the United States," May 2002, page 1.

140. U.S. Department of Health and Human Services, National Institutes of Health, National Institute on Drug Abuse, "Research Report on HIV/AIDS," March 2006, page 1.

141. U.S. Department of Health and Human Services, Substance Abuse and Mental Health Administration, "Results from the 2008 National Survey on Drug Use and Health: National Findings," September 2009, page 6.

142. Ibid.

143. National Drug Control Strategy, Office of National Drug Control Policy, "2009 Annual Report," January 2009, page 7.

144. Office of National Drug Control Policy, "The Economic Costs of Drug Abuse in the United States, 1992-2002," December 2004, page x.

145. U.S. Department of Health and Human Services, Substance Abuse and Mental Health Services, "Worker Substance Use and Workplace Polices and Programs," June 2007.

146. Ibid, page 4.

147. "Cocaine use among U.S. workers declines sharply in 2008, according to Quest Diagnostics Drug Testing Index. " press release, May 6, 2009.

148. U.S. Department of Health and Human Services, Centers for Disease Control and Prevention, Motor Vehicle Safety, "Impaired Driving," January 26, 2009, page 1, see: http://www.cdc.gov/MotorVehicleSafety/Impaired_Driving/impaired_-drv_factsheet.html.

149. Walsh, J.M., Flegel, R., Cangianelli, L.A., Atkins, R., Soderstrom, C.A.,, Kerns, T.J., "Epidemiology of alcohol and other drug use among motor vehicle crash victims admitted to a Level-1 trauma center," Traffic Inj Prev, 2004;5:254 - 60.

150. Ch'ng, W., Fitzgerald, M., Gerostamoulos, J., Cameron, P., Bui, D., McCaffrey, P., Drummer, O., Potter, J., Odell, M., "Drug Use in Motor Vehicle Drivers Presenting to an Australian, Adult Major Trauma Centre," Emerg Med Australas, 19 August 2007, (4):359-65.

151. Beirness, D.J. and Beasley, E.E., "Alcohol and Drug Use Among Drivers: British Columbia Roadside Survey 2008," Canadian Centre on Substance Abuse, Ottawa, ON, 2009.

152. Laumon, B., Gadegbeku, B., Martin, JL., Biecheler, MB., "Cannabis intoxication and fatal crashes in: population based case-control study," BMJ, 10 December 2005, 331(7529):1371. 1293-1296.

154. Ibid.

155. National Highway Traffic Safety Administration, "Traffic Safety Facts Research Note," U.S. Department of Transportation Report No. DOT HS 810 821, Washington, D.C. 2007.

156. U.S. Department of Health and Human Services, Substance Abuse and Mental Health Services, "Results from the 2008 National Survey on Drug Use and Health: National Findings," September 2009, page 29.

157. National Institutes for Health, National Institute on Drug Abuse, "Drug-Impaired Driving by Youth Remains a Serious Problem" news release, 29 October 2007.

158. Department of Health and Human Services, Substance Abuse and Mental Health Administration, Office of Applied Studies, "Children Living with Substance-Dependent or Substance-Abusing Parents: 2002-2207," April 16, 2009.

159. Ibid.

160. The National Center on Addiction and Substance Abuse, Columbia University, "Family Matters: Substance Abuse and the American Family," March 2005, page 2.

161. Ibid.

162. National Drug Intelligence Center, National Drug Threat Assessment, "The Impact of Drugs on Society," January 2006.

163. University of Maryland, Center for Substance Abuse Research, CESAR FAX, Vol. 18, Issue 16, "Methamphetamine Cost Society an Estimated $23 billion in 2005; Majority of Costs Related to Addiction, Premature Death, Crime and Criminal Justice," April 27, 2009, see: http://www.rand.org/pubs/monographs/MG829.

164. U.S. Department of Health and Human Services, Substance Abuse and Mental Health Administration, "Results from the 2007 National Survey on Drug Use and Health: National Findings," September 2008, page 55.

165. Marin Institute Fact Sheet: The Costs of Alcohol, June 24, 2008.

166. As of April 1, 2009.

167. See http://www.CDC.gov/tobacco.

168. Office of National Drug Control Policy, "National Drug Control Budget: FY 2010 Funding Highlights," May 2009, page 2.

169. U.S. Department of Education, "Fiscal Year 2010 Budget Summary -- May 7, 2009," accessed May 20, 2009, at www.ed.gov/about/overview/budget/budget10/summary/edlite-section1.html.

170. Department of Health and Human Services, Substance Abuse and Mental Health Administration, Office of Applied Studies, "Drug Abuse Warning Network, 2004: Area Profiles of Drug-Related Mortality." 2008

171. Johnston, L.D., Bachman, J.G., and O'Malley, P.M., "Monitoring the Future: Questionnaire Responses from the Nation's High School Seniors." Institute for Social Research, 1980.Page 266.

172. Johnston, L.D., Bachman, J.G., and O'Malley, P.M., "Monitoring the Future: Questionnaire Responses from the Nation's High School Seniors." Institute for Social Research, 1992. Page 327.

173. Foulkes, Imogen. "Ten years on from Needle Park". February 4, 2002. www.swissinfo.ch.

174. U.S. Department of Health and Human Services, Substance Abuse and Mental Health Administration, Office of Applied Studies, "Drug Abuse Warning Network, 2004: Area Profiles of Drug-Related Mortality," 2008.

175. Johnston, L.D., Bachman, J.G., and O'Malley, P.M., "Monitoring the Future: Questionnaire Responses from the Nation's High School Seniors," Institute for Social Research, 1980, page 266.

176. Johnston, L.D., Bachman, J.G., and O'Malley, P.M., "Monitoring the Future: Questionnaire Responses from the Nation's High School Seniors," Institute for Social Research, 1992, page 327.

177. Foulkes, Imogen, "Ten years on from Needle Park," February 4, 2002, see: www.swissinfo.ch.

178. Ibid.

179. Department of Health and Human Services, Substance Abuse and Mental Health Services Administration Office of Applied Studies, "Results from the 2008 National Survey on Drug Use and Health: National Findings," September 2009.

180. U.S. Department of Health and Human Services, National Institutes of Health, National Institute of Alcohol Abuse and Alcoholism, "Rethinking Drinking: Alcohol and Your Health," publication no. 09-3770, February 2009.

181 U.S. Department of Health and Human Services, National Institutes of Health, National Institute of Alcohol Abuse and Alcoholism, "Rethinking Drinking: Alcohol and Your Health," publication no. 09-3770, February 2009.

182 Mokdad, A.H., Marks, J.S., Stroup, D.F., Gerberding, J.L., Actual Causes of Death in the United States, 2000, JAMA 2004, 291(10):1238-1245.

183. U.S. Department of Health and Human Services, Public Health Service, National Institutes of Health, National Institute on Alcohol Abuse and Alcoholism, "10th Special Report to the U.S. Congress on Alcohol and Health," June 2000.

184. U.S. Department of Health and Human Services, Centers for Disease Control and Prevention, National Center for Chronic Disease Prevention and Health Promotion, Office on Smoking and Health, "Women and Smoking: A Report of the Surgeon General," Atlanta, GA, 2001.

185. U.S. Department of Health and Human Services, Centers for Disease Control and Prevention, "Annual Smoking-Attributable Mortality, Years of Potential Life Lost, and Productivity Losses—United States, 1997-2001," Morbidity and Mortality Weekly Report 2005: 54(25) 625-628.

186. U.S. Department of Health and Human Services, Centers for Disease Control and Prevention, National Center for Health Statistics, "Health, United States, 2005, with Chartbook on Trends in the Health of Americans," Hyattsville, MD, 2006.

187. U.S. Department of Health and Human Services, Centers for Disease Control and Prevention, "Smoking-Attributable Mortality, Years of Potential Life Lost, and Productivity Losses—United States, 2000-2004," Morbidity and Mortality Weekly Report 2008, 57(45):1226-1228.

188. U.S. Department of Health and Human Services, Centers for Disease Control and Prevention, National Center for Chronic Disease Prevention and Health Promotion, Office on Smoking and Health, "Sustaining State Programs for Tobacco Control: Data Highlights 2006," Atlanta, 2006.

189. "The Tax Burden on Tobacco," Historical Compilation, Orzechowski and Walker, Volume 43, 2008, Arlington, VA.

190. Federation of Tax Administrators, "State Excise Tax Rates on Cigarettes, January 1, 2008," Washington, D.C., 2008. State excise taxes ranged from 7 cents in South Carolina to $2.58 in New Jersey.

191. U.S. Department of the Treasury, Alcohol and Tobacco Tax and Trade Bureau, "Tobacco: Federal Excise Tax Increase and Related Provisions."

192. Heron, et al, "Deaths: Final Data for 2006," U.S. Department of Health and Human Services, Centers for Disease Control and Prevention, National Vital Statistics Reports, Vol. 57, Number 14, April 2009, DHHS Pub No (PAS) 2009-1120 (Tables 21 and 22), see: http://www.cdc.gov/nchs/data/nvsr/nvsr57/nvsr57_14.pdf.

193. Department of Health and Human Services, Substance and Mental Health Services Administration, Office of Applied Studies, "Results from the 2007 National Survey on Drug Use and Health: National Findings," September 2008.

194. Department of Health and Human Services, Substance and Mental Health Services Administration, Office of Applied Studies, "Results from the 2008 National Survey on Drug Use and Health: National Findings," September 2009.

195. Rosenthal, Mitchell, "Panacea or Chaos? The Legalization of Drugs in America." January 15, 1993

196. U.S. Department of Justice, Office of Justice Programs, Bureau of Justice Statistics, "Drug Use and Dependence, State and Federal Prisoners 2004," October 2006, revised January 2007.

197. Gruber, A.J., Pope, H.G., Hudson, J.I., Yurgelun-Todd, D., "Attributes of long-term heavy cannabis users: A case control study," Psychological Med, 33(8):1415–1422, 2003, see: http://www.nida.nih.gov/infofacts/marijuana.html.

198. Lezin, N., Rolleri, L., Bean, S., Taylor, J., "Parent-child connectedness: Implications for research, interventions and positive impacts on adolescent health," ETR Associates, Santa Cruz, CA, 2004.

199. O'Malley, P.M., Johnston, L.D., "Drugs and driving by American high school seniors, 2001–2006," J Studies on Alcohol and Drugs, 68(6):834–842, 2007.

200. Gruber, A.J., Pope, H.G., Hudson, J.I., Yurgelun-Todd, D., "Neuropsychological performance in long-term cannabis users," Arch Gen Psychiatry, 58(10):909–915, 2001.

201. The National Center on Addiction and Substance Abuse, "Family Matters: Substance Abuse in the American Family," Columbia University, March 2005.

202. Goldman, Salus, Wolcott, Kennedy, "A Coordinated Response to Child Abuse and Neglect: The Foundation for Practice," U.S. Department of Health and Human Services, Office on Child Abuse and Neglect, User Manual Series (2003), see http://www.childwelfare.gov/pubs/usermanuals/foundation/foundatione.cfm.

203. U.S. Department of Justice, Office of Justice Programs, Bureau of Justice Statistics, "Criminal Victimization, 2007," see: http://www.ojp.usdoj.gov/bjs.abstract/CV07.htm.

204. Crime in the United States, 2006." Murders that occurred specifically during a narcotics felony, such as drug trafficking or manufacturing, are considered drug related.

205. U.S. Department of Justice, Office of Justice Programs, Bureau of Justice Statistics, "Drug Use and Dependence, State and Federal Prisoners 2004," October 2006, revised January 2007.

206. U.S. Department of Justice, Office of Justice Programs, Bureau of Justice Statistics, "Criminal Victimization in the United States, 2005," Statistical Table No. 32, NCJ 215244, December 2006.

207. U.S. Department of Justice, Office of Justice Programs, Bureau of Justice Statistics, "Substance Dependence, Abuse, and Treatment of Jail Inmates, 2002," NCJ 209588, July 2005, and "Drug Use and Dependence, State and Federal Prisoners, 2004," NCJ 213530, October 2006.

208. Califano, Jr., Joseph A., "Should Drugs be Decriminalised? No." BMJ 2007, 335:967 (10 November), doi:10.1136/bmj.39360.464016.AD.

209. U.S. Department of Health and Human Services, Substance and Mental Health Services Administration, Office of Applied Studies, "Results from the 2008 National Survey on Drug Use and Health: National Findings," September 2009.

210. U.S. Department of Health and Human Services, Center for Disease Control and Prevention, "National Vital Statistics Report, 2005," Vol 56, Number 10, April 24, 2008.

211. National Drug Control Strategy, Office of National Drug Control Policy, "National Drug Control Strategy Data Supplement 2009."

212. National Highway Transportation Safety Administration, "Traffic Safety Facts, 2007," DOT HS 810 985.

213. Department of Health and Human Services, Substance and Mental Health Services Administration, Office of Applied Studies, "Results from the 2007 National Survey on Drug Use and Health: National Findings," September 2008.

214. National Highway Transportation Safety Administration, "Traffic Safety Facts, 2007," DOT HS 810 985.

215. U.S. Department of Health and Human Services, Substance and Mental Health Services Administration, Office of Applied Studies, "Results from the 2008 National Survey on Drug Use and Health: National Findings," September 2009.

216. European Monitoring Centre for Drugs and Drug Addiction, "2008 Annual Report: The State of the Drug Problem in Europe," Office for Official Publications of the European Communities, Luxembourg, June 2008, page 11, see also www.emcdda.europa.eu.

217. Ibid.

218. Ibid.

219. Simons, Marlise, "Cannabis Cafes Get Nudge To Fringes of a Dutch City," New York Times, August 20, 2006.

220. "Cannabis Bars in Limburg to be for Members Only," NIS News Bulletin, May 13, 2009, see: http://www.nisnews.nl/public/130509_1.htm.

221. Collins, Larry, "Holland's Half-Baked Drug Experiment," Foreign Affairs, May/June 1999, p. 87.

222. MacCoun, R., Reuter, P., "Interpeting Dutch Cannabis Policy: Reasoning by Analogy in the Legalization Debate," Science, 278, 47-52, 1997, see: http://ist-socrates.berkeley.edu/~maccoun/scienc97.html.

223. Report of the International Narcotics Control Board for 2005, International Narcotics Control Board, United Nations, New York, 2006, p. 84.

224. "Amsterdam Bans Smoking of Marijuana in Some Public Places," Expatica, January 29, 2007, see: www.expatica.com/actual/article.asp?subchannel_id=19&story_id-5804.

225. Hibell, B., Guttormsson, U., Ahlström, S., Balakireva, O., Bjarnason, T., Kokkevi, A., Kraus, L., "The 2007 ESPAD Report - Substance Use Among Students in 35 European Countries," the Swedish Council for Information on Alcohol and Other Drugs (CAN), Stockholm, Sweden, 2009.

226. "Netherlands from 12th to 5th Place in Europe on Cannabis Usage," NIS News Bulletin, April 4, 2009, see: http://www.nisnews.nl/public/040409_1.htm.

227. "Cannabis: An Apology," The Independent on Sunday, 18 March 2007, see: www.news.independent.co.uk/uk/health_medical/article2368994.ece.

228. "UK: Cannabis to Be Reclassified as a Class B Drug," 8 May 2008, see: http://www.scoop.co.nz/stories/WO0805/S00105.htm.

229. "Cannabis is Now a Class B Drug," UK Home Office press release, 26 January 2009.

230. Cohen, Roger, "Amid Growing Crime, Zurich Closes a Park it Reserved for Drug Addicts, " The New York Times, 11 February 1992.

231. "Drug Use by Europe's Young People Leads to Risky Sexual Behavior," Medical News Today, 1 August 2008. see: http://www.medicalnewstoday.com/articles/116883.php.

232. European Monitoring Centre for Drugs and Drug Addiction. "2008 Annual Report: The State of the Drugs Problem in Europe," Office for Official Publications of the European Communities, Luxembourg, June 2008, see: http://www.emcdda.europa.eu.

233. Office of National Drug Control Policy, "Who's Really in Prison for Marijuana?" NCJ 204299.

234. Mumola, C.J., "Special Report: Substance Abuse and Treatment, State and Federal Prisoners, 1997," Department of Justice, Bureau of Justice Statistics, January 1999, NCJ 172871.

235. Ibid.

236. Ibid.

237. Office of National Drug Control Policy, "Who's Really in Prison for Marijuana?" NCJ 204299.

238. Mumola, C.J., "Special Report: Substance Abuse and Treatment, State and Federal Prisoners, 1997," Department of Justice, Bureau of Justice Statistics, January 1999, NCJ 172871.

239. Office of National Drug Control Policy, "Who's Really in Prison for Marijuana?" Executive Office of the President, Office of National Drug Control Policy, NCJ 204299.

240. Ibid.

241. Ibid.

242. U.S. Sentencing Commission, "2008 Sourcebook of Federal Sentencing Statistics," see: http://www.ussc.gov/ANNRPT/2008/SBTOC08.htm, Table 33, http://www.ussc.gov/ANNRPT/2008/Table33.pdf.

243. "Behind Bars: Substance Abuse and America's Prison Population," National Center on Addiction and Substance Abuse (CASA) at Colombia University, January 1998.

244. U.S. Sentencing Commission, "2008 Sourcebook of Federal Sentencing Statistics," see: http://www.ussc.gov/ANNRPT/2008/SBTOC08.htm, Table 33, http://www.ussc.gov/ANNRPT/2008/Table33.pdf

245. National Drug Crime Institute, see: www.ndci.org/courtfacts.

246. Roman, et al, "Recidivism Rates for Drug Court Graduates: Nationally Based Estimate – Final Report," The Urban Institute and Caliber, Washington D.C., 2003.

247. Fluellen, R., Trone, J, "Issues in Brief: Do Drug Courts Save Jail and Prison Beds?" Vera Institute of Justice, New York, NY, May 2000.

248. United Nations Office on Drugs and Crime, UNODC and Drug Treatment Courts ("Drug Courts").

249. Rempel, M, Fox-Kralstein, D., Cissner, A., Cohoen, R., Labriola, M, Farole, D., Bader, A., and Magnani, M., "The New York State Adult Drug Court Evaluation: Policies, Participants, and Impacts," Center for Court Innovation, New York, NY, 2003.

250. "A Cost-Benefit Analysis of the Saint Louis City Adult Felony Drug Court," Institute for Applied Research, St. Louis, MO, 2004.

251. "To Treat or Not to Treat: Evidence on the Prospects of Expanding Treatment for Drug-Involved Offenders," The Urban Institute, 2008.